CEO SPEAK: LESSONS FROM BUSINESS LEADERS

Profitable Customer Relationships

Top CRM Experts Reveal the Secrets of Creating Customers for Life

VISION BOOKS

(Incorporating Orient Paperbacks)

New Delhi • Mumbai • Hyderabad

www.visionbooksindia.com

ISBN 10: 81-7094-624-7
ISBN 13: 978-81-7094-624-3

First Vision Books Edition, 2005
Reprinted, 2008

Originally published as *Profitable Customer Relationships*
www.aspatore.com

Published by
Vision Books Pvt. Ltd.
(Incorporating Orient Paperbacks and CARING imprints)
24 Feroze Gandhi Road, Lajpat Nagar-III,
New Delhi-110024, India.
Phone: (+91-11) 2983 6470 ; 2983 6480
Fax: (+91-11) 2983 6490
E-mail: visionbk@vsnl.com

Cover Design by hatchdesign.org

Printed at
Rashtra Rachna Printers
C-88 Ganesh Nagar, Delhi 110092, India.

Contents

CEO SPEAK: LESSONS FROM BUSINESS LEADERS

"Real world advice from real experts"

This internationally acclaimed series provides real world lessons from C-level business leaders (CEO, CFO, CTO, CMO, Partner) from some of the world's most respected companies. Each chapter is a future-oriented look at the most important issues for success. Every contributor has been carefully chosen for his or her proven business expertise in order to give readers actual insights from the thoughts, perspectives, and techniques of accomplished professionals worldwide. Because so few books or other publications are actually written by executives in industry, this series presents an unprecedented look at contemporary issues never before available.

"What C-Level executives read to keep their edge and make pivotal business decisions. Timeless classics for indispensable knowledge." Richard Costello, *Marketing Communications, General Electric*

"Want to know what the real leaders are thinking about now? It's in here." Carl Ledbetter, *SVP & CTO, Novell, Inc.*

"Unique insights into the way the experts think and the lessons they've learned from experience." MT Rainey, *Co-CEO, Young & Rubicam/Rainey Kelly Campbell Roalfe*

"A valuable probe into the thought, perspectives, and techniques of accomplished professionals. By taking a 50,000 foot view, the authors place their endeavours in a context rarely gleaned from text books or treatises."

Chuck Birenbaum, *Partner, Thelen Reid & Priest*

"A great way to see across the changng marketing landscape at a time of significant innovation."

David Kenny, *Chairman & CEO, Digitas*

"True insight from the doers in the industry, as opposed to the critics on the sideline." Steve Hanson, *CEO, On Semiconductor*

"What the bigwigs read."
Paul Simons, *CEO, Ogilvy & Mather, UK*

"Become an expert yourself by learning from experts."
John Ferver, *Co-Founder, Advertising.com*

"An insightful read for those who want to gain insight . . . lifetimes of knowledge and understanding." Anthony Russo, *PhD, CEO Noonan, Russo Communications*

"A tremendous treasure trove of knowledge . . . perfect for the novice or the seasoned veteran." Thomas L. Amberg, *CEO, Cushman, and Amberg Communications*

"Real advice from real experts that improves your performance immediately." Dan Woods, *CTO, Capital Thinking*

"Easy, insightful reading that can't be found anywhere else."
Dominick Esposito, *Vice-Chairman, BBO Selidman*

"A must read for anyone in the industry."
Dr. Chuck Lucier, *Chief Growth Officer, Booz-Allen & Hamilton*

"A rare peek behind the curtains and the minds of the industry's best." Brandon Baum, *Palmer, Cooley, Godward*

"Captures the essence, the deep-down thinking processes of people who make things happen." Martin Cooper, *CEO, Arraymann*

Starting from Scratch

Richard Brock
Firstwave Technologies, Inc.
Chairman & CEO

Developing a Profitable Customer Relationship

Developing profitable customer relationships is the key to business success. Profitable customers appreciate what you're doing for them and will serve you in return. Great products, great companies and great business leaders are defined by their ability to develop profitable relationships. As a CEO, I find most of my time and energy is devoted to acquiring and maintaining relationships, which will serve this company beyond the life cycle of our current solution. These relationships are truly the lifeblood of our existence.

But, to properly develop profitable customer relationships and achieve the blue ribbon of customer success — customer loyalty — a company must start from scratch. Competitive and product principles need to be evaluated and aligned. Employees must understand that a job well done is only well done if it benefits the customer's business and the customer relationship. This means teaching your employees how to understand the customer, their business processes and their customer acquisition strategy.

The introspection required to acquire and develop loyal customers is arduous, but it is the methodology by which your company differentiates and succeeds in the marketplace. Anyone can have customers, and it's even possible to have customer relationships. But, a company with a long-term market strategy can't simply be a vendor —

they need to be a partner, with partner-based relationships that are profitable.

Acquiring New Customers

Introspection — A Look Before You Leap

While a majority of effort and time are spent on marketing and selling to potential customers, the success of those efforts is rooted in a company's customer acquisition philosophy. Congruent to a corporate philosophy, this philosophy is the cornerstone for how a company will compete for customers in the marketplace.

Possibly the most interesting book on the subject, *In Search of Excellence* by Thomas J. Peters and Robert H. Waterman, Jr., defines three ways you can compete to gain customers: operational excellence, product excellence, or customer intimacy. The book makes the point to choose one and let that lead your company. Another choice may be a secondary goal, but you can't pursue all three. For example, if you're Home Depot, you compete with the lowest price based on operational excellence; if you're Neiman Marcus, you compete with the best service. If you're Intel, you compete with the best technology.

At Firstwave, we focus on customer intimacy (best service). That means that we focus on companies that are searching for a business partner to provide a comprehensive solution to help them solve specific problems and develop customized applications. It means that we have to say we don't just provide out-of-the-box applications; we provide integrated solutions. Not that technology can't be shrink-wrapped, but people who want an out-of-the-box application only don't want to buy from a vendor who is focused on delivering a solution. It affects your pricing, marketing, delivery model, and everything else.

After laying the foundation for your competitive strategy, the most important step to developing a solid customer relationship is to establish credibility as someone who cares about that relationship. Essentially, you are not only a salesperson, but a truly effective partner in solving a business problem. The customer has to know that you have integrity and you will be blatantly honest about your abilities. Based on that honesty, you will seek those opportunities where you fit best. Before you make a proposal for business, you have to earn the right to do so. If you gain the confidence of the customer based on personal integrity, you develop a valuable relationship. If you develop a relationship, it means the customer finds you valuable to their company.

Personal Integrity Requires an Introspective Analysis of Your Company, namely Your Employees

Every employee must focus on customer retention and customer satisfaction — this is priority number one. Furthermore, you must instill a sense of ownership and pride with your employees, so that if they misrepresent anything about the product or fail to gain the customer's confidence, then they know it will reflect upon them personally and professionally. This keeps everyone honest, and customers will be confident that you are a true partner. For your product or company to be successful, there must be people confident in your integrity, whether that is because of your product, your competitors, your price, your service, or a combination of all those things. It's a matter of honestly focusing and aligning goals.

One of the problems in the software industry is that for years the focus was on new account selling. Those companies that focused solely on reaching for the next new deal are experiencing the consequences of their actions. This focus does not add value to any relationship because it compromises both credibility and integrity. If you don't believe in your product or service, if you don't focus on long-term retention, if you just want a quick sale with the cheapest service and cheapest product out there, it is not possible to have a relationship. You have to inspire the sales staff through compensating a job that is not only done, but one that creates a valued relationship that outlasts compensation.

Laying the Foundation for a Long-Lasting Partnership

There are three steps to begin a long-lasting relationship with a customer. It starts by identifying their core problem. It is a listening mode. We meet with them to help us understand why they called us, find out their perceived problem and what efforts they've already made to address the problem. The bottom line is people like to open up — and this establishes confidence. Even more important, it establishes a partnership approach to solving the customer's problem.

So, step one is to listen so that you truly understand the requirements. The second step is to repeat the requirements so they are confident that you understand them, and step three is to talk about your solution in light of their requirements. That begins to develop a relationship and starts to separate you from other companies who don't really care who the customer is or where their problem stands, just the available budget. There are too many people out there who do that. But, of course, that's the opportunity for the rest of us.

Here at Firstwave, we prefer to have partnerships with our customers. To do that, we rely on the three steps above to open the lines of communication, honestly set expectations, and communicate our value to the customer's organization. Customers expect Firstwave to solve a problem. We listen to their problem, understand how they feel, and then provide the solution. That's what we do and it is what they expect from us.

Firstwave routinely goes through a process called a gap analysis as a part of each sale. We enumerate the customer's requirements and needs, and have a working session. We get the users involved, because they usually know more of the details than the people on the screening committee. We then can say here is how we understand your requirement, and here's your solution. Determining the gap between what they want and what we offer is a very detailed, step-by-step process. The gap analysis is also a key part of establishing appropriate customer expectations.

All that we expect from the customer is honesty in the relationship. It's important that they give us the proper feedback and fully participate in the partnership. If they're not happy with our service, I would ask them to say so and allow us to address it. A customer is generally unhappy because you didn't set the right expectations going in. Perceived value is truly the heart of the matter — if people are unhappy with your price, maybe you're in the wrong business. But assuming you're not in the wrong business, you have most likely not communicated your value proposition that justifies your price.

Referrals — Testimony to Walking the Walk

One of the best ways Firstwave has been able to sell its vision is through our customers. We've had several sales where a person came to us because they were impressed with our sales support system being used by a company that was trying to sell them their product. Their impression of our solution was so positive that they wanted to buy that system for their own organization. It's being the best example of what you do, walking the walk. We use our CRM solutions internally, which instills internal confidence and experience in your company's product. This is vital to gaining the confidence of your customers.

A referral, such as the example just described, is the best beginning to a new relationship. A customer or partner referral allows you to have initial meetings on a higher-level than you would otherwise because you're not being screened. Instead, you're being perceived as a company of value that can help, and you're being invited in to help discover their requirements and how your product can meet their needs. In essence, without even having made the sale (which will most likely happen), you have become a partner.

At Firstwave, if we acquire a customer correctly, we realize a greater success factor. We expand with their business as they expand, and we expand to other divisions in their company. More importantly, when they go to one of their tradeshows or seminars, they may be talking over a cup of coffee with someone who is looking for a similar system, and they suggest to that person that they should try their vendor-partner. That is the right way to do business.

Customizing Communication and Solutions to Achieve Results

Each person conducts business differently, and we all respond to different stimuli. Some people want an e-mail channel, some want a phone channel, some want to visit you, and others want you to visit them. Therefore, I think the communication channels you use initially depend upon whichever channels are preferred by the customer. You then modify the channel based on whether the initially chosen channel was successful. It's like a restaurant. You offer meat, fish, vegetables and starches, but in the end you serve what people buy. Similarly, when acquiring new customers, you must offer the normal communication channels, and then listen to the customer and find out what he or she wants.

Customization must be addressed on two fronts. As described above, you must tailor your communication channels to reach individual customers. But, you must also offer product or solution customization.

In customer relationship management, if you have the same business processes as your competitors, then you have no competitive advantage. The biggest company will win because of the lowest cost of production. Establishing a competitive position takes strategic tailoring. So we have record keeping systems, if you will, and those can be homogenous. They are contact management systems, and they are part of our basic solutions. You have to have that capability to work "out of the box." But when you get into the business rules and business processes, and the escalation and workflow rules, that's what makes CRM really valuable. Of course, this all varies from company to company, so an effective solution that addresses these rules and issues must be customized.

Building Customer Loyalty

Customer Retention versus Customer Loyalty

While customer retention may result from a relationship, customer loyalty should be the desired result. Customer retention equates to someone who is simply using your product. Customer loyalty means that you have earned the customer's trust and confidence. While a loyal customer expects you to be competitive, your business is not always at risk because they view you as a strategic partner, rather than a vendor. Customer loyalty doesn't mean that you serve that customer for the initial life of that particular product, because people may buy things to use for a little while. Customer loyalty means that they buy their subsequent products from you because you are their partner.

For example, if you're an automobile manufacturer, you want a customer to buy the first model of a particular car, but then also the succeeding models. For instance, my brother bought his first Saturn, and they were so successful in the way they treated him, that he has purchased two more. That's customer loyalty — it stems from the successful relationship. A loyal customer is not only confident and impressed by how a solution was reached, but has now decided there is no need to re-evaluate the relationship from a competitive standpoint. It means that you are the source they come back to so that they can grow.

Delivering Quality Customer Service

Similar to the previous section on acquiring customers, building customer loyalty requires us to first look inward. At Firstwave, we recognize that to build loyalty we have to deal with people on both sides of the equation. This means you need to gauge your customer support staff, as well as gauge customer perception.

For example, I had one support manager review a questionnaire for customers who have called in support. The list of inquiries included items such as: Was the person interested in solving your problem? Did the Firstwave employee have the technical knowledge and competence to solve your problem? The support manager got upset with the survey and said that these customers were not qualified to evaluate his technical competence. Unfortunately, he didn't understand, so I found a new support manager. It's the customer's opinion that counts.

We conduct these surveys to allow us to recognize what the customer perceives to be true. It's all about the customer's perception. You can say that the support managers really do help the customers until you're blue in the face, but until we have the quantitative feedback, which is directed back to me as the CEO of the company, it does not matter. These surveys provide an example of what the customer wants. People like attention, but they really expect results. If you're a doctor who has a bad bedside manner, even if you get positive results from an operation, the patient won't come back to you. On the other hand, if you are a very nice, friendly doctor, but the patient dies on the table, that's not a very good result either. What we do is address both sides of the coin: remain focused on the customer solution and recognize the importance of customer perception.

Empowering the Customer

Loyal customers are confident partners in your company. As a partner, we feel that it is our duty to empower our customers with more than CRM solutions. We have to also empower them with problem-solving techniques that will allow them to fully understand the benefits of what we bring to the table. It's a win-win situation — our value is better communicated and customers have confidence in their ability to maximize how well our solution works for them.

A past goal at Firstwave was to reduce the number of support calls we received. Through surveys, we realized that many of our calls were the result of customers failing to use the help documentation and training manuals. So, we developed a new strategy, which has achieved two goals: reducing our support calls, and more important, empowering our customers with the ability to solve their problems.

Our first tactic was to introduce a shift delay in our response to support calls. In other words, when a customer call comes in, their question is logged in to provide tracking and then directed to the most appropriate support manager. That manager then returns the customer's call within five minutes and provides them with the answer.

This process has multiple purposes. First of all, the most appropriate person contacts the customer. It shows our desire and care, and eliminates any room for error. Second, the waiting period has statistically and dramatically reduced the number of calls. In the past, people found that calling the support line would provide an immediate response, as opposed to having to look up the answer in the manual. By introducing the five-minute delay, customers would be more inclined to first find the answer in the manual. But, if they did not find the answer, or they chose not to look in the manual, we were able to get the most knowledgeable person on the phone. This helped us reach our goal and, more importantly, we helped the customers help themselves, resulting in increased confidence in our product.

There is a definite danger in giving too much technical support and therefore not empowering the customer — this is human nature. Human nature states that a person will always want to show off how smart they are. Therefore, a support person or manager might tell a client to type in a lot of highly technical computer code (read: intimidating) to fix the problem, but that shows they didn't have any confidence in the product. It is more important to show the product structure, and work through the product's documentation, which has defined the answer. If the support person gives the client a "geek shortcut," then the client becomes dependent on the support staff. The staff member, on the other hand, thinks he's doing the customer a favor, but really, he's giving them a fish instead of teaching them how to fish. Interestingly, he's also inadvertently setting the client up to believe that the product is not easy to use.

In order to ensure that our support managers were assisting the customers in solving the problem, we added a box on the support call log that required the manager to point out the page number where this item was described or addressed in the manual. This way, if the "cool" support guys aren't properly addressing support complaints, we can confront them. We don't alienate them, but deal with it fairly, inquiring whether they knew that the issue was covered on a particular page. In reality, they didn't know the page number, because they hadn't read the documentation. They were techies, so they didn't need to read the documentation. But they were cheating the customers. So by forcing them to enter the page number on their logs, they had to know the documentation. Then they would give the customer the page number, the customer would look at it, feel good about it, and the call would end positively. Both sides win in this kind of customer relationship.

Customer Support Challenges

One of the greatest customer support challenges is dealing with companies who did not opt to adequately train their workforce on your solution. This results in a high number of customer support calls. We have a system in place to alert us to extraordinarily high calls from one customer. When this happens, we call them and we go not to the person who is calling, but to the person who signed the contract. At this point, we discuss the situation and ask how we can help fix the situation. More often than not, this person hasn't heard anything because he or she bought it and moved on.

We then go on to explain that while you have hundreds of customers using this package, last week you received 22 calls from this particular company, which represented 10 percent of your calls. You suggest that you haven't done a very good job of training their people, and therefore offer some reduced-fee training, or even free training, to help clear up the problem. You take the stance that your training clearly was not adequate. Instead of suggesting that the customer's employee is not competent to do their job, or the person who understood the system left, you suggest that it might be your fault. You step forward and ask the company to allow you to service this problem.

Basically, we have taken this aberrant problem, which is an untrained person, and turned the relationship around. We initiated the call because we have the system in place to ring a bell that this problem is aberrant. You suggest that the fault is partly yours, and take full responsibility in doing so. We offer a solution, and instead of you being unprofitable because the company is calling too frequently for support, they will realize our fairness and won't take advantage of us. The customer apologizes for the turnover, and subsequent lack of training, and then the profits come back into the relationship and they are probably a better customer and a better reference.

Impact of New Technologies on CRM

Separating the good customer relationship management applications from the not-so-good applications is generally very simple. A product has to be easy to use, intuitive to use, and it has to be available when you need it. No matter how you slice it, if it's not easy to use and not available where it's needed and when it's needed, then it's not going to work. That's the whole secret. New technologies have greatly impacted these basic principles of CRM application success.

I have been in the business for more than 18 years and feel the Internet has made CRM really effective because it is easy to deploy and use. But, while the Internet has improved CRM, I think that it has also screwed up the "local business advantage" because each customer has access to a world of information and options. This translates into a far more efficient market, where people know who has what at what price. Price, geography, and market inefficiencies are no longer issues to deal with. The real focus is on customer satisfaction, which means that you are going to have to serve your customers if you are to compete.

One of the biggest changes in the CRM field right now is the advent of the new tablet PC and the PDA (Personal Digital Assistant). If you're going to be a customer intimate company, you have to have the details on hand. We've seen, however, that in the past, no one would use a standard PC or laptop in front of a customer because it was unnatural; the rep couldn't type fast enough, he was distracted, he wanted to look them in the eyes, and therefore, he usually wanted to take handwritten notes. Information really wasn't captured in the step that it should have been. The new convertible tablet PCs are a tremendous help. You can, in fact, use them in meetings because they allow you to take free-form notes.

There is an 80/20 rule that says 20 percent of the people will use the handwritten recognition properly, while 80 percent will just scribble on a pad, but that's what they would be doing anyhow. So, we now have character capture versus character recognition. I believe with the easy-to-use character capture, the people will use it to attach those notes to the customer with whom they're talking. We have improved the salesperson's efficiency, because the notes are in their proper location. Twenty percent of people will do the handwriting to text translations. But 80 percent of the time, people will expect them to have captured the notes, which is how we have been doing business. The current generation of these devices is going to replace the pen and paper. And that's pretty powerful.

Major changes are often realized by reaching tipping points. This is where something is good, but when you add it to something else, it gets that much better and it just takes over. Case in point, we can think back to the digital Rolodex. They did not really take off until the Palm Operating System was developed and put to use. Palm gave us a calendar and the personal digital assistant with all of our names and addresses. More importantly, they decided to sync it with our e-mail system. Palm would not have worked without e-mail. E-mail caused people to create databases on their personal computer. Because they had those names and addresses in the personal computer, Palm's secret was to link this information into the little device, and people realized that they could have the calendar, with all of these names and addresses whenever they need them. Furthermore, everybody realized that if you ever had the discipline to put all of that information into the digital Rolodexes, one day the battery crashed or it got rolled over by a chair and you lost everything. Then you realized the same thing could happen with your notebook computer. But, since you can easily synchronize it to your Palm device, the Palm device and my notebook back each other up on key information.

Then PDAs really started getting legs under them when they came out with the phone attached. When you call me, I recognize your phone number because it brings up your name. When I call you, I can look up your name and press "dial" and I don't have to dial the number. Convergent devices are powerful in terms of having information at your fingertips; plus they're always on, which is a main reason why the notebooks are not used. So, you can scribble the handwritten notes of the sales meeting, which is very good, and you don't have to recast them except to attach them. It's no different than what would happen before, but now it's all organized and you take better notes, because the notes are where you need them when you need them.

Another technology tipping point that will change how we work is WiFi, or Wireless Fidelity, which is basically a wireless local area network. You can enter a Starbucks, for example, and pay a couple of dollars and have high-speed Internet access if you have a WiFi card in your PC. Most of the PCs today are shipping with WiFi in the computer as an added benefit. You can pay a few dollars at airports, and have access to it, and you can have WiFi in more and more hotels and other venues.

If your office has WiFi capabilities, I can walk into your office and begin working on a virtual private network from my home office and have total network security while accessing sensitive information such as my e-mail. Furthermore, I can now work flexibly with my customers by being able to perform such activities as checking the status of their account receivables or their inventory, in a manner which is convenient and time-efficient.

The data, which is important in the relationship, is the next step. It's all about the workload and information going back and forth. Information lubricates a good relationship. In the near future, you're going to start to use your notebook, because you're using it in the meeting itself to scribble your notes. You're capturing your notes in real-time; you've also already put this information in your enterprise database because you're using your customer's WiFi connection to do all of this in the background. This is big medicine; it's a big change. Also, if you take the right enabling technology, you can comprehensively view a customer and all the pertinent data that affects both your business and theirs. In this view, you can bring up accounts receivable, which might be in Chicago. Or you might need to access the mainframe in Miami, which has all of the maintenance information. The orders are kept in an Oracle database in Oregon, and your sales are kept in a database in Seattle. Basically, you can bring up a composite screen in front of the customer in real-time view of all these disparate data sources. You can see the back orders, things that just happened, and the current status. A whole bunch of enabling technologies are dramatically changing the way we do business.

To take the success of these technologies further, I think you have to focus on customization capabilities so these technologies can better fit their needs. CRM technologies have to be easy to customize and easy to use. That's the answer. If it is easy to customize and easy to use, everything else will take care of itself.

Success in the CRM Field

You minimize the risk by knowing what you're doing. It's like flying airplanes, motorcycle riding, or scuba diving. You shouldn't be too risky because sooner or later, you will lose. If you take a risk, you should control and manage the risks of that decision to make sure the odds are stacked in your favor. You need to quantify your risk and eliminate risk with low pay-off. If you go into markets where the nature of the product being sold is totally opposite to what you stand for (i.e. "stack them high and sell them cheap"), you're moving away from profitable opportunities.

You must begin by finding your kindred spirits. Find a customer who is dedicated to their customer because you are dedicated to the customer. Birds of a feather flock together. Basically, when you get into a sales situation, if you see that this company is looking for product, but they don't appreciate your unique selling proposition, you're probably not going to change them. So, the best decision for both parties is for you to get out of the relationship. You have to understand what it is you want to get into. I had a friend who parachuted. He was very good at it and then one day, he was parachuting and the wind was dangerously strong. Lo and behold, he parachuted anyway and broke his ankle horribly because he pushed the envelope. He knew he shouldn't parachute when the wind exceeds a certain speed. My advice then is to know your limits; know where your sweet spot is and stay there.

Rule number one: if you don't take care of your customer, someone else will. That's our motto. Rule number two doesn't exist. What I have learned from my experience is that you have to have a perceived value to initially get a sale. But then you have to offer real value to sustain a relationship. That's why you have to market properly, sell properly, and support outrageously to gain customer loyalty and profitable, long-term relationships.

Named one the 10 Most Influential People in CRM by Sales and Marketing Automation *magazine, Richard Brock founded and serves as Chairman and CEO of Firstwave Technologies, Inc. Firstwave, a pioneer in the Sales Force Automation market and a leading provider of web-based Internet Relationship Management applications, was started by Mr. Brock in 1984 to address the needs of companies seeking a complete solution to automate their sales, marketing and customer service. His entrepreneurial spirit has resulted in Firstwave establishing an international presence and serving over 200 companies in 20 countries.*

Mr. Brock has also played a significant role in the development and management of several companies. He founded Brock Capital Partners, a capital investment firm, and is a director of Datastream Systems, Inc., a leading provider of maintenance software. Prior to his originating Firstwave, Mr. Brock founded and served as CEO of Management Control Systems, a software provider for CPA firms that is now a division of Research Institute of America. In addition, he has held board positions with three other companies.

Formerly the Chairman of the Technology Association of Georgia, Mr. Brock has assumed numerous industry leadership positions and has received many accolades through his entrepreneurial career. He has served as President and Board Member of the Business & Technology Alliance, President of the Entrepreneur's Division and Board Member of the Information Technology Association of America, President and Board Member of the Southeast Software Association, Chairman of Georgia High Technology Month and Board Member of the Technology Executives Roundtable. He was named Georgia's High Technology Entrepreneur of the Year in 1990.

A Certified Public Accountant, Mr. Brock received his MBA from Louisiana State University and his BS from Spring Hill College.

The Profitable Ecosystem of Customer Relationships

Gregory J. Hanson
Bullhorn, Inc.
CEO

Developing Profitable Customer Relationships

Developing a profitable relationship with a customer starts at the first contact. We approach our customers with the attitude that we're entering into a partnership, and it's a long-term relationship from which we should both profit. If these relationships are started with that attitude, ultimately both parties end up benefiting. So the conversation initially revolves around, "What are your needs, and do we have something that fits your needs?" We are as much looking to fit with them as they are with us. Because we're selling a service as much as a product, this initial conversation forms the backbone for all our efforts from that point forward. Ideally that philosophy pervades our relationship throughout the lifecycle with the customer — through the sale, the implementation, the billing cycle, the service, and finally, the customer relationship.

Our client companies expect our system to work perfectly 100 percent of the time — it needs to be secure, stable, accessible, scalable, easy to use, relatively inexpensive, and constantly improving. When you put all those things together, that's a pretty tall order. Customers expect to be able to reach us whenever they want to; as long as they can do that and get some sense that someone somewhere is working on their issues, whether it's a new idea or a problem, then they're fairly satisfied. And I think on a business level they expect us to be flexible. Some of them will want us to be flexible on billing; some will want us to be flexible on service offerings; some will want us to be flexible on pricing.

We expect to deliver all of that and more. Customers are demanding, but we believe that the best product and service doesn't just meet the demands at a point in time, it meets demands over a long period of time. We don't expect customers to provide us with the next generation of technology. We expect to come up with that ourselves. We don't expect them to pay for a service or product that's not satisfactory, but we do expect them to work with us when it isn't. We expect some level of communication from customers. We try to provide a high level of communication, so we expect the same from them. And although we don't expect it, we encourage them to share their experience with others, ideally, when it's good. Other than that, we expect them to be able to focus on their business and not worry about what we're doing. If everything works perfectly, they shouldn't have to think about our system at all. It's kind of like the lights or the electricity in your apartment: it does what you need it to do, what you expect it to do.

In our little part of the world, I think the difference between good solutions and great solutions is that great ones can continue to evolve as customers evolve. That's a simple way of saying something that's enormously complex in practice. Evolution can be technical development, a change in pricing, a service modification. I think the reason there was a gap created for us to enter this market is that older software vendors in our industry didn't evolve in a way that would allow their customers to deal with the Internet revolution. The other vendors had evolved in a way that would improve their own profits, but hadn't evolved with their customers' ultimate success in mind. I think that as long as we keep our customers' success at the forefront of our minds, we will continue to provide a great solution. It may sound a little too altruistic — it's not; we're in this for profit — but if you believe that you can only be as profitable as your most profitable customer, then I think everybody wins and we will prevail over others who don't see this. As already mentioned, we look at our customers as partners, and all the feedback loops and self-referential issues start with the first contact. We definitely are not a passive player in the process.

We drive the relationship as much as we can. But at the end of the day, you need that company to be profitable or they're not going to be much of a customer for long.

We also promote strong customer relationships by aligning our basic business with customers. It seems to us that right now in our particular market, our customers' goals in this economic environment are to continue being able to offer a variety of services to their own customers easily and quickly and maintain their margins. Our goals are essentially the same, although we're their vendor. So there's a little bit of a synergy between the way we look at our customers and the way our customers look at their customers. I think that synergy is not exactly a primary driver, but it's very informative to always keep that in mind, because it basically allows for an open conversation with our customers about what we need to do in order to service them adequately. That may mean we build new tools, or revise our contract, or revisit some element of our service that the customer did or did not purchase, or any one of a number of things.

The sanctity of the customer relationship is tremendously important. Our revenue goals and operating goals and so on are outside of how we deal with customer relationships, and we try to make sure that things going on within the company — say, financing, or growing the employee base, or making changes in the organizational structure — don't disrupt the primary relationship with customers. And keeping that alignment sacred is a very key thing.

We measure our customer relationships relentlessly. Referrals and attrition rates are indicators of success. We work in a relatively close-knit industry, and high-quality referrals — people who are sending us their business partners or friends — are very important. Contract renewals are important as well. We look very carefully at attrition of any kind, whether it's just shrinkage or a customer leaving or choosing something else. We look at all of those things, not only at the point of first contact but all the way through the process of the company being a customer some time in the future. We feel that if our customers are benefiting, then we're going to benefit. We will always want to sell them as much as we possibly can that will fit their business, and if we think we have a fairly significant contract opportunity that ends up not being so large, that's like attrition. Or if we have a customer that starts at a large size and then ends up at a smaller size later on, we also look at that as attrition. So those are all measures of our success.

I think a huge misconception is that you have to make every customer happy. We work very hard with our customers, but there are such things as bad customers, and we do let them go. We offer to point them in a direction we think would be better for them, and that's because we think that bad customers can drain huge amounts of resources and detract from our ability to service good customers.

We believe we have a great deal of control over good customers versus bad customers. A good relationship starts at the first contact. A good customer is realizing some significant value from our product and service, and as long as that's the case, there's usually a very good match. If they're not realizing any value, then we either sold them something we shouldn't have, or they purchased something they didn't need, or there's some sort of mismatch. I think a good customer, when receiving value, is more than willing to pay and to refer business, and will directly benefit — hopefully their whole business will benefit.

Flexibility is important. To paraphrase a very funny movie clip, "whatever the customer says today is already outdated, and tomorrow they'll want something completely different, and what they want now is really what they wanted done yesterday." Overall the landscape and the technology is changing quickly, and you have to be very flexible and quick on your feet to keep up with everything. I think that's a very important characteristic of companies that can sustain profitable customer relationships over time.

Honesty, perhaps above all else, is very important in a strong customer relationship. Integrity is incredibly important. If anybody in our company says we'll do something, we will do it, and that may mean we take a loss. I think it's unacceptable to not produce things that you claim to produce. You have to be very honest about what your capabilities are. And I think that also goes to the question of what is a bad customer. Sometimes you just have to be honest with yourself about not being able to provide what they may need, and say, "Can we help you find the right solution?" That's also an institutional thing; you have to really, really demand that people have high integrity.

The best piece of customer relationship advice is two-fold. First, there are good customers and bad customers, and you should focus on the good ones and try to cut links to the bad ones. Second, there are external customers and internal customers; the external customer is a traditional customer, and the internal customer is an employee. The combination of those two facts dramatically affects the business. If you view your employees as customers, and you pay attention to them and their success in the way that you pay attention to your own external customers, you will dramatically outperform the company that's not thinking that way. If the function of customer relationships is to create profits and grow the business, then I think those two pieces of advice are orders of magnitude more significant than any other piece of advice I've ever received.

Internally, the discussion I most often have with employees is that we need to focus on our customers' success, and we need to provide an honest evaluation of our capabilities and their needs as early as possible in the process, because that creates the groundwork for everything else we do. And externally, I promote similar concepts, the first one being that our customers' success is intimately tied to our own success, because the more successful our customers are, and the more profitable, the more profitable we are. We are absolutely 100 percent focused on our customers' generating value from our products and services. And that's probably the most significant message I share externally.

Challenges

It's constantly a challenge to efficiently match the expectations of customers with the realities of our service and our product. We like customers to come on board with us with a very clear understanding of what they're getting, and that's always a challenge. In the sales process, it's tempting to overstate or oversell or provide the best-case scenario. So as a company, we look very carefully at what customers expect, and we constantly evaluate if there's a new requirement surfacing that we should plan for, build for or provide for. It's a constant challenge, really. And as our existing customers' businesses change, we need to keep pace with them, and the challenge is to proactively get them to tell us what's going on, rather than waiting for them to call us and say, "Something's changed; we're going elsewhere." We really try to be extremely proactive, because by the time they come tell us, it's probably too late. Our basic strategy is to try to understand what the fundamental nature of the change is — whether it's something to do with the service we're providing, or if it's something more core to their business, which we can't affect. For example, if one of our customers' major industry sectors has collapsed and their business has shifted dramatically, that's a macroeconomic change that we can't control. We're not business consultants, so we wouldn't be able to help them with that. But one of the things we can do proactively in that kind of situation is to help them understand how our system can allow them to think more creatively about their business, or to change direction if they need to, and just help them be aware that those options are there if they choose to use them.

Staying on top of knowledge is another challenge. It's a combination of just trying to poke around in every source that I am familiar with, but I try to keep an ear to the ground for things that people are saying, either directly or indirectly, or off-handedly. And I try to cultivate a sense in other people around the company that they should do the same, so that that filters to me. It's hard. It's a challenge because there are so many other things going on.

I think one of the ways that we have managed to keep ahead institutionally here is that the backgrounds of the people in our company are extremely diverse, and they look at problems, solve problems, and gather information very differently. That's a massive advantage, because if you have cookie-cutter employees who all look at things the same way, I think you end up with a singular way of solving problems, and that's not really helpful. We value a plurality of ideas. I think that's been one of the keys to our success, both with the business model and the product and sense of the industry and so on. There's no hard-and-fast rule, but I like to look for unique experiences — maybe not core to the job function they're going to be doing, maybe adverse kinds of experiences. We have helicopter pilots and retail salespeople and scientists and engineers and consultants and recruiters and all kinds of crazy backgrounds. The trick is that when you're looking at people you're looking past the specifics to get at what the general underlying ability is. It's a hard thing. It's not 100 percent effective. We definitely take risks on employees, and some work out and some don't.

Customer Acquisition and Retention

We engage primarily in direct sales efforts. We will contact individuals at companies on a targeted basis. We know a great deal about our industry and the way companies function and the way the market is segmented, and we primarily work in that industry. There's a strictly sales-oriented communications targeting strategy, and then there's a corporate communications targeting strategy. Opportunistic things do happen, of course: people contact us from out of the industry and ask us about our software. But generally what we do is direct sales. Our goal is basically to talk to every single company in the industry several times a year — not as a hard-core sales effort, but just, "We're out here. What's going on with you?" One of the reasons we do that is because we believe the market is so dynamic and fast-changing that they don't know what's going to be happening six months from now, so the best thing for us is to just keep talking to them — not in an aggressive "I want to sell to you or never talk to you again" kind of way.

For ourselves, we define complete customer acquisition when we have signed a long-term contract with a customer and they are up and running on the system and sufficiently satisfied that the implementation requirements have been met. It basically means we have a lock on their business. It's not an easy thing for a company to switch off of our system, because it covers so many parts of the business. We don't make it difficult; it's just that we usually take over three or four of their systems and breaking from our system into several others is much harder than one would imagine. So, as far as our customers are concerned, they acquire a new customer when they staff a position at a client, either on a temporary or a permanent assignment. And it's not that different from what we consider customer acquisition. They acquire the customer when they make that placement; we acquire the customer when we implement our system for their business. So there's a bit of symmetry there as well. Ideally for them, they would have plenty of repeat business from the same customers, and we look at it the same way. We hope they grow and add users to the system, and then that's like repeat business for us.

Our system makes the process of making a placement for the staffing company very easy: it's very easy to track, it has very few steps, it's very rigorous, and they can customize it to their own process. That is the exact same benefit that we provide in terms of covering loyalty to them. They essentially get very good oversight on their accounts where they've made placements, and they can keep tabs on their customers to a fine degree and service their customers with these ongoing relationships in a very fine way. They can offer additional services, and they can see into the account activity very easily; it's all rolled up in one place. And we use the exact same tool ourselves to track our customers, because again, there's a similarity between what our customers are providing their customers and what we are providing our customers. We use our own system to provide the best possible service to our customers and therefore drive loyalty.

So along the acquisition-loyalty-retention line, our system will give them the ability to view what customers have requested, what their behavior has been like in the past, what other things are going on in their company. Retention with staffing companies really revolves around keeping up with the times and being able to be quick on their feet and responsive to requests. They're really providing a service, and our system has direct access to all the service issues that arise at the client. Outside sales will know what's going on inside a customer while recruiting and management will know if new opportunities are rising or falling. This kind of oversight enables up-selling and cross-selling, for example, and drives retention. This supports loyalty, new acquisition and so on, so in some ways it's a self-fulfilling circle.

Again we use the same system as our customers and are very focused on being proactive and having detailed real time information about every account.

The ideal customer life cycle is when we find them, we sell to them, and we keep them forever. But realistically, the ideal customer life cycle is one where we find them or they find us, and there's a relatively short period of time in which they already know they need a solution. They choose us as their solution of choice, they fully understand what we can provide, and they move into implementation. As time goes on, they add modules to the system, they ask for new features — which benefit other customers, which benefit our products, which benefit them — and they grow, and they're profitable, and they stick with us for many years. We sell a managed service, so ideally there's no end to it. It's not like building a product on spec and selling it, and the customer goes away and maybe comes back later. So we would really like to retain all of our customers. And the ideal thing is that the employees of our customers move to other companies and spread the word of our system to those companies.

We have a two-tiered sales and account management or sales and implementation system. The sales effort morphs into an account management effort during the process, so the lead salesperson who closes the contract will provide oversight and be a point contact forever with that client, and our revenue and our sales are annuity-based, which provides an incentive for the salesperson to stay in contact with the client and keep them happy and growing. That's the first internal driver. As far as the customer is concerned, because of that incentive on our side, the customer receives constant communication at various levels, both at the upper account management level and the lower tech support or help desk level. We're very aware of what's going on at that company. We have many details — automatic reports about what parts of the system they're using, how often, what users are doing — and all of these things are available to anyone in the company in real time, and it's a very sophisticated technical and overlapping operational process that keeps our eyes and ears on every customer.

We are constantly releasing new features into the system, and those don't all become available to every customer. Some are optional and some are mandatory, but they're usually all free as part of what our system allows. It's like a utility in that if the water department improves the quality of the water, you automatically start to gain that benefit at home. And with things that would actually effect how the user interacts with the system, we will communicate that both at the account-management level and then also at the end-user level so that everyone knows what's coming when and if it matters to them and why it matters, and so on. And then we also collect feedback all the time about new feature requests and ideas. We often will just build something right into the product; everybody benefits. So there's a bit of an ecosystem of ideas, and I think that's one of the keys to our "profitable" customer relationship. If we're adding value to them and they automatically add value back to us, then this is one of those examples of the feedback loop: the more value we add to them, the more they add to us.

How Customer Relationships Will Evolve

In the near future, if not already, I think customers relationships will become much more demanding for vendors and that the level of communication and specificity, the responsiveness, the detail, and so on — essentially, the level of service — will all increase. Customers will continually become more and more educated about the things they're buying. I think this is essentially a function of the service economy. In every sector of the economy, the consumers' education level, generally speaking, is increasing, and that is driving an increased demand on the customer service level. The most successful companies, not just the biggest ones, will provide very tailored, very specific, very valuable customer service, and they will be miles ahead of the ones that don't. The days when you call a nameless, faceless service representative somewhere and wait on the phone for 30 minutes are nearly at an end. You call any company now and give them an identifier, and they know your name, they know everything about your account, they know your entire history with them. It's incredible. I think that is just going to become a requirement, not just a "nice to have."

Imagine the company that can service a complex customer base with a minimum of expense, not because the product is simplistic or the customers are all forced to interact with the company through touch tone phones, but because they have advanced systems for accepting all kinds of customized requests. Imagine the individuality, specificity, responsiveness, and detail of a medical exam applied to basic customer service. The companies who do this will completely overwhelm companies that don't cater to the customer. Customers know there is choice in the market and customer service at this individualized level is the ultimate retention and loyalty tool.

Gregory Hanson joined the Bullhorn team as the Senior Vice President of Product Development and was the principle product designer for the two-enterprise applications that Bullhorn has brought to market including BullhornSTAFFING™. He was instrumental in developing the strategy to target the multi billion-dollar Staffing and Placement Industry and it was his vision that enabled Bullhorn to create what is now an industry leader in this vertical market.

Prior to Bullhorn, Mr. Hanson was founder and managing principal of PLY L.L.C., an architecture and interactive design/consulting firm in Michigan specializing in multidisciplinary services to commercial, institutional, and private clients. Mr. Hanson has also served as an Adjunct Lecturer at the University of Michigan Taubman College, a computer specialist in the Solar and Stellar Physics Division at the Harvard-Smithsonian Center for Astrophysics. He has published numerous peer-reviewed articles and discovered a galaxy, G272.2-3.2, in the southern hemisphere. Mr. Hanson is the recipient of several awards for research, design, and interdisciplinary leadership.

The Key to Profitable Relationships

Michael Silton
Rainmaker Systems
CEO

At Rainmaker, we're focused on the service agreement, so our goal is to drive more service revenue and to drive that revenue more efficiently. To do that, we help companies build relationships with their customers on an ongoing basis through direct marketing, telephone sales, and Web and e-mail commerce. In other words, our services help companies increase the lifetime value and profitability of their customer relationships.

The key to a long-term profitable relationship with a customer is thinking not only about the initial sale but also about the long-term relationship. When a customer buys a product, it's just the start of the relationship. Customers invest time and thought in their purchase decision — that's an investment in the product and the company that makes the product. With technology products and consumer products — and just about everything these days — customers want a return on that initial investment paid out over time through a relationship with the vendor. How you, as a vendor or manufacturer, manage that ongoing relationship will determine whether that customer is going to be profitable in the long term, for two key reasons. First, the way you treat a customer in servicing their existing systems will determine whether or not they recommend your system to other people, and also whether they are likely to buy additional services or products from you later. Second, the actual service relationship itself can be profitable. Most companies have looked at service as a necessary evil — something they need to provide to keep their product working so that customers will buy the product in the first place. But if you focus on what your customers need and provide the right service offerings, you can deliver profits on an ongoing basis from your customers. So, as your company grows and you gain more and more customers, you can develop more and more profit, and service becomes a profit center rather than a cost of doing business.

With a focus on long-term relationships with customers, you can measure your success in a variety of ways. One of the key areas that we look to is service contract attachment rates and service contract renewal rates. If you have a customer who buys a product, and there's a service contract available, their purchase of that contract indicates a higher level of relationship — they want to stay engaged, they're planning to use the product, and so forth. So if a customer buys a service agreement at the point of purchase or soon after, you have an ongoing relationship right from the start. Then, when you want to sell additional products or services, you're already in the relationship; you're not trying to recreate one. Another key area to look at is the renewal rate. If a customer who has a one-year service agreement decides to renew again for the next year, you're actually learning several things. You're learning that the value you provided for that service contract was positive, and they want to continue that. So you had a good relationship and a good service offering. The second thing you're seeing in the renewal is that the customer is planning to continue to use your product, and that tells you that your product itself is of value to that company on an ongoing basis. That speaks well for selling more products to that customer, or selling them future products as well. You need to look at what percentage of customers buy service contracts up front, and then what percentage renew. And it's important to look, not just at the dollar amounts of the renewals that you get, but also at the unit renewal rate. Because if it's just the large customers that are renewing, and many of your small customers are not renewing, your dollars on a percentage basis might look good but the reality is that you're losing a lot of your customers every year. So you need to look a level deeper.

The third key measurement is dollars of service revenue per customer. Most companies have several levels of service agreements, and we find in most cases that the majority of the customers have base service contracts, whatever the lowest level is. That's because it's the easiest, and when you're focused on getting the initial sale, you don't want service to look complicated. So the base service agreement is sold. But if you're looking at that profitable long-term relationship in which your customer is happy because they have the right level of service, not just the cheapest — and some customers want higher levels of service and are willing to pay for it — then you're able to see the total dollars that you're bringing in per customer. Typically, if you've priced your products and services correctly, you will be more profitable at the premium levels of service and your customers will actually be happier with the premium levels of service.

Determining a customer's future profitability is usually based on what patterns they set. So the first thing you need to understand is which of your existing customers are most profitable, and develop that profile. Most service organizations today, when asked who their most profitable customers are, will either point to their largest customers or some other general characteristic. But if you can delve into another level deeper and understand what the real profile of those customers is, then you can find more of those customers. But typically in a services organization, it's the product group that's driving what your prospects are. If someone buys the product, then you have an opportunity to sell the service agreement. If a services organization can help determine what kinds of customers are most profitable in the long run, and show that they can actually make as much money on the service contract as they made on the actual sale, they can help drive the strategy of the new product sales to target more of those particular customer sets.

I believe customer relationships are undergoing a dramatic transition right now. Traditionally, customer relationships have been focused on a product and a one-time sale, and then occasionally additional product sales down the road. Relationships are now switching to services. It's an ongoing, continual relationship. You have a customer; you want to keep that customer for life. That's the most profitable way to run a business. It's what leading services organizations are building into their strategies. It's also what customers are starting to expect. So switching from the mindset of creating and delivering products to managing an ongoing relationship around the customer and the services they're receiving is a dramatic shift. It requires different ways of doing things and different ways of building relationships.

A Foundation of Communication

Good relationships have several key foundations, including open communication and trust. Open communication is really about two-way communication. It's not only sharing with your customers what your plans for the future are, so that you're building a common ground, but it's also about listening to your customers. If you start by listening to what their needs are, what their concerns are, what their plans are, you'll be in a better position to support your customer going forward. If you communicate with your customers about what your plans are, they'll feel better about the relationship. It's that open communication that builds trust over time, and when there's trust, then your customer will feel comfortable about staying in a relationship with you. You'll feel comfortable sharing your true needs and not just negotiating. A solid long-term relationship requires ongoing dialogue. You can never have a relationship with a person if you don't even talk to them. To look at it from a more personal perspective, your best friends are people you can trust, and how did you build that trust? You built it over time, through interactions, through listening, through sharing, and you had to share personal things about your future, and they shared things that you listened to. That combination of two-way communication and an open environment builds trust, builds relationships. The stronger the relationship, the better chance you have of having the right products and services going forward, and the better chance you have of keeping those customers happy.

One of the key starting points in building a successful long-term services relationship is recognizing that it's an ongoing relationship. It's not a one-time sale of a product. It's not "let's call up every time we need to get some money from our customer." It's a relationship, and a relationship is about listening and communicating, and not just communicating about money. Most companies today focus on their service relationships in two ways. One is when someone calls for support, and they answer the phone, and the other is when it's time to get money, and they make a phone call. If you had a relationship where the only time you spoke with the person was when you called them, or when they needed something from you, that's not going to build a great relationship. Those aren't your best friends. You want someone who calls you to build the relationship when it's not about something they need.

How do you do that? At Rainmaker, we do a couple of things to help companies manage their service relationships. The first is to tell them, "Go and communicate with your customer and find out what they're thinking at a time when you're not asking for money." So if you've got a year-long service contract, maybe at the six-month point you send out a survey. This is something that we do with many of the service contracts that we manage for companies. We learn a couple of things. We uncover any problems that the customer may have. The advantage of that is that if we uncover an unsatisfied customer — and they do exist from time to time, for whatever reason — we're then able to help solve that customer's problems. And if the customer is taken care of then, when we ask them for money later to renew their service agreement, all they remember is the positive experience. If we didn't know they were unhappy, however small the unhappiness was, when we contacted them three or four months later to ask them for money for their service contract for the following year, and then they told us they were unhappy and then we resolved it, the chances of them renewing are much lower. The reason for that is the customer's perception. In the first example, the customer says, "You took care of me. I had a great experience. Now you're asking for money; of course I'm going to renew." In the second example, they say, "You took care of me, but you only took care of me when you wanted something from me." Again, it's a subtle change in the relationship, but that's the kind of difference between a great customer relationship and a relationship with a customer who is buying your services just because they have to.

Now, there's a second benefit to proactively going to your customers during the course of their service agreement when they haven't called you. In most companies today, there's turnover. And turnover occurs in two ways: people change companies and people change roles in a company. So the same person may be there, but they may have a different responsibility. Often, a new person coming into a job doesn't have all the transition information they would like. A new person coming into a job may not even know they have a service agreement. So a person comes into a job; six months later they get a call from a company saying, "We're here to renew your service agreement." The person didn't know they had a service agreement. They've lived without it for six months because they didn't know they had it, so they found some other way to keep their systems running. They aren't likely to want to pay for it next year because they lived just fine without it. But if you found that person and made sure they knew they had that service agreement six months earlier, they might have taken advantage of it, or at least known it was there as a security blanket and not found a way to solve potential service issues, so when you ask for the money again, you're more likely to get it. So to deal with high turnover rates, proactively going to those responsible for a service agreement at the mid-point of the year or at some other time during the length of the contract helps you uncover the people who don't know they have a service agreement.

A business-to-business relationship is still a relationship. There are people involved. The fact that you think you're communicating with a company doesn't change anything — if that person is either not there or not listening, one-way communication is not going to produce any results. In today's world, where e-mail and one-to-one communications can be managed efficiently with the right systems, you have the opportunity to do this for all your customers — your large customers in person, and your medium and small customers electronically — and stay in touch with those people who manage the relationship with you and understand their changing needs.

One of the important things to keep in mind in a business-to-business relationship is that communication needs to be about finding the right people at the right time with the right messages. And you have to have all three of those. It's not just a single person, usually, when you're dealing with a business-to-business relationship. And in complex service agreements and in other longer-term important high-value relationships, it's not about a single communication or a single medium. In an ongoing relationship, it's not just one message. The messages have to change and vary and be the right ones at the right time, so they can get that two-way open communication and trust. If you keep in mind the right people, the right messages, and the right timing, you're going to have effective, open, two-way communication, and that's the key to an ongoing relationship.

I think the key to being proactive in a relationship is that most customers today expect lousy service. They expect that they're going to buy something from you and they'll never hear from you again until you want more money from them. That's the expectation, so they're not going to call you just to build the relationship. It's up to the company to be proactive and build that relationship, and show that they see value in the ongoing relationship — not just the short-term revenue.

The second part is just reacting and listening — whether it's listening to your customer's preference for media (what kind of communication they want, and would they prefer to hear from you by letter or by e-mail), what kinds of services or products they are interested in, what's their experiences with the support offerings, and so on — so that you can improve not only the relationship but your service offerings going forward.

A rich, happy personal life is based on having strong, trusting personal relationships. In the business environment, a rich, profitable company also has multiple strong, open, trusting relationships with its customers. It's not enough to say you love your customers. It's about communicating and listening, consistently, as a core element of your business operations.

Developing Customer Strategy

Maximizing a company's service revenue all starts with the data and the customers. Most companies don't have great customer records when it comes to the service relationship, because often the person who bought the equipment isn't the same person responsible for deciding on the service relationship. And most companies, especially large ones, keep customer information in several different systems. So the first challenge is to get a good picture of the customers and the service agreements that are out there. What percentage of customers is not covered? What percentage of customers could be on a premium level of service that isn't today? What percent of customers aren't renewing every year? Once you have an understanding of the landscape — the quantity of customers and the revenue opportunity, an understanding of your customers and what abilities you have to communicate (via direct mail, e-mail, and other forms of communication), you can get a sense of the best approach to maximize revenue for that customer base.

Once you understand who they are, what the opportunity is, and how you can communicate with them, you need to listen. That means going to customers one on one or in groups, in person or by direct marketing, to hear what their responses are. This can be done through conversation or, more effectively, through pilots. You come up with some theories about what would drive increased customer satisfaction and increased revenue, and you pilot it with a customer segment and see what happens. The beautiful thing about direct relationships and direct marketing is the direct feedback they generate. If you set them up right, direct programs can give you tangible results that tell you the quality of your customer relationships. Direct programs are also exciting because they encourage experimentation of new ideas — new offers, new prices, new messages, new customer segments. Everything is just a matter of trying it and seeing what works. This has been our experience at Rainmaker — we've tested thousands of different ideas and forms of communications and special offers and promotions — to see what's most effective and what customers are most interested in, so we're able to bring that existing knowledge to bear right from the start, and then continue to refine approaches that are unique to a particular company.

The Role of Technology

Technology isn't a substitute for a customer strategy — it plays a huge role in helping a company execute its customer strategy. We've all seen examples of companies investing millions in sophisticated customer management systems with very disappointing results. The reason these companies fail isn't the technology — it's the lack of experience applying the technology to their business needs. Until you apply technology to an important business need, especially when you talk about Web technology and e-mail and Internet communication, until you put it up and have actual customers doing something with it at a sufficient volume, you don't actually discover what's going on. So the experience I'm talking about is real customers — really interacting. Why is Amazon.com one of the best websites around, one of the easiest to use? It isn't because they have the best technology. They do have great technology, but they didn't say, "Let's just have the best technology"; they stopped and listened and watched their customers' experience. With every transaction they learned, and with every customer comment they learned, and they went out and solicited customer comments. If you're a company that is looking to leverage technology to manage your service contract sales, you can go buy great technology, but if it's not tested and working in the real world, adapting and improving every day, you're going to get great technology but a bad customer experience. What you want to find is technology that has been applied to your area of need, technology that has the experience built-in.

Another success factor for using technology is the process and the people that you have in place to deal with the exceptions. I think about that, especially in the Web area. If you have a Web customer experience, you might think, "We're going to automate it. We're going to put all these wonderful features in, and it's going to be the best Web system ever in the world." That's great, and it's going to work 99 percent of the time, maybe even 99.9 percent of the time. But that 1 percent of the time, or 0.1 percent of the time, when it doesn't work makes all the difference. I could go to your Web site every day and have a great experience for 364 days in a row, and if on day 365 I have a bad experience, I'm going to fume. But when I'm stuck or frustrated, whether it's the technology's fault or not, if you give me a simple way — like an 800 number on that Web page — to talk to a live human who's not only empathetic but who's energetic, and who listens to what I have to say and is empowered to do something about it, then I have a great experience and I'm back to the Web site the very next day. If I have a bad experience, I may never come back. So the best technology is technology that has great people around it to make sure that the 1-in-100 time when something does go wrong, or isn't prepared for, or isn't part of the normal process, you can be taken care of and you're not left alone. It comes down to relationships. You can't automate your relationships. You can automate your interactions much of the time, but you have to provide a way for real people to talk to real people.

The customer doesn't want to know that they're interacting with different technologies. They want to interact with the company. The technology is there to help that relationship. So to make the technology efficient, the ability to move information about the customer between systems needs to continue to develop. New tools like XML and some of the standards around are steps in the right direction, but we certainly have a long way to go to really make that work well.

The systems also need to mature. It's not about always getting to the next step in terms of technology; it's about making sure the technology is addressing the customers' issues. In an ongoing relationship, that's about listening to their needs. Back to Amazon — I can't point to one example of the biggest technology change that Amazon had implemented in order to better serve its customers. What I point to is a series of small, steady steps that incorporated their experience and made a difference. And if technology can continue to take an incremental approach to improvement, rather than just looking for quantum leaps, I think customers will be better served. In the end, the full potential of technology as a tool to help companies increase the profitability of their customer relationships depends on whether a company is prepared to make a commitment to ongoing customer communications as part of their broader customer strategy.

Michael Silton is CEO of Rainmaker Systems, a leading outsource provider of sales and marketing programs for service contracts. His vision for Rainmaker is to help technology companies overcome the serious challenges they face in building better and more profitable customer relationships while staying focused on their core business.

Prior to Rainmaker, Mr. Silton led marketing at MAI, a large hardware manufacturer with an extensive services organization. Before that, he was COO of a leading provider of ERP solutions to soft goods manufacturers. His early career included management roles at software publishers and resellers.

Customer Focus

Beatriz V. Infante
Aspect Communications
Chairman, CEO & President

Long-Term Profitable Relationships

Our business and our vision are to fundamentally change how businesses interact with their customers, suppliers, partners, and their own employees. We do that by providing the technologies that enable companies to drive a customer strategy.

A customer relationship overall and in an aggregate needs to be profitable and long term. You may pass through phases in which it isn't profitable in the short term, but the total lifetime value of the customer to your business is really the key to the long-term profitability of your business.

Keeping customers in a long-term profitable relationship is much easier than it might seem. There are a small number of key principles that can be demonstrated with an example from our own business. First, you have to decide that you are a customer-focused business. The first and foremost and fundamental principle is that you are not market-share focused or technology focused but customer focused. You have to buy 100 percent into the idea that if you get the right customers, provide the right quality of goods and services to them, and do certain things to keep the bonds strong, then they will stay with you. The total lifetime value of those customers will be well worth the extra effort.

The second point is key in a business-to-business environment, which is what we are in. In a business-to-business environment, it is absolutely crucial that your business treat the customer's staff as individuals and not merely as representatives of a larger corporate entity. You have to have that personal touch. To illustrate this point, let me give you an example from one of our great customers, Washington Mutual. They have made tremendous strides in the banking business over the last several years, and they have done that by focusing on the personal touch. For them, that personal touch is important even with their technology vendors. They are very much a modern day banking phenomenon. They have made 33 acquisitions in the past 20 years, which is amazing, and they are still known for treating their customers well and presenting one face to customers despite the challenges associated with mergers and acquisitions.

We, Aspect, were already providing contact center solutions to many of the companies that Washington Mutual had acquired. We took great care of each individual who worked with each of our products at each site. As a result, as these acquisitions were completed and Washington Mutual had to standardize on contact center technology, the people we had embraced who championed us within their particular companies then championed our solutions within Washington Mutual. As a result, over the many years that Washington Mutual has been a customer, their total value to us totals in the tens of millions. They continue to spend heavily with us for sophisticated technology that helps them to present that single face to their customers. They are a reference account for us. They are a customer-partner. They send people to speak to our employee meetings and tell them how much that relationship means to them. They attend our trade shows with us. The point is that by treating the individuals that make up Washington Mutual as individuals first and corporate representatives second, we now have people who have built a career on our solutions and promote them as they move along in their own careers. Lesson? Never underestimate the true power of loyalty and treating customers fairly.

It is that level of loyalty that leads to long-term profits. Did it cost us any more to treat our customers that way? No. In fact, many times, it has actually saved us money because they are forgiving and loyal supporters. For example, on one occasion we had a product that wasn't quite ready for Washington Mutual's scale of deployment. Our account rep told them that. He told them that it was a great product and that they needed to standardize on it, but that at their size and scale, they should wait a year. He suggested, "Why not let other companies that are smaller and that have more focused deployments become successful? Let's make sure that the software is really solid for you." Now Washington Mutual is buying that product from us on a large scale because we told them ahead of time that it was more of an early adopter product, and that at their scale and size they weren't quite ready to deploy the product yet. That type of situation takes a lot of trust and treating the person on the other side as an individual and understanding their risk and respecting their commitment goes a long way. Sounds simple, yes, but it is harder to do than you might think — especially if your business is not solidly driven by customer-focus.

Third, to have strong relationships with your customers and generate long-term profit for your company, you really have to know who the customer is and understand what is in the best interests of the company and also of your individual internal champions. If you make your internal champions successful and the parent company successful, you will win in the long run. Sometimes that means pushing them to take a risk, and sometimes that means saying that you don't want to take that risk and making that decision with them as a partner. When you do that, they remember it, and they trust you afterward when you make a recommendation. If your recommendation doesn't quite work out, then they come back to you with greater trust because they have been a partner in that decision-making process. They don't immediately assume that you are trying to sell them something quickly and not really understanding their interests or their business. It is very possible to have long-term relationships and very profitable relationships, but you have to start with that customer-focus first.

Aligning Goals

The first thing we have to do — and this starts with the sales force and the technical specialists in our sales organization as well as with our consulting group — is to understand the customer's mission before we begin to analyze the situation. It isn't just what their business objectives are. We start with their mission. With Washington Mutual, they told us very clearly that their vision is one voice, one customer service experience. That is a very succinct statement of a very broad set of principles that drive every business decision at Washington Mutual. By understanding that ultimate goal, we then were able to put all of their business requirements in perspective.

We spend a lot of effort and do a lot of up-front research with new customers to see if and how our solutions can really address their business problems. We also assess whether the potential customer has a goal of really supporting their customers, employees, and partners, or if they just want to get in quick and engage in a short-term business relationship. Frankly, we walk away from the latter. There have been situations in which it has become obvious that the customer that we were attempting to sell to was really not looking for a partner relationship. They wanted a vendor to sell them something very cheaply. They were going to turn around then and deploy it very quickly. They themselves did not have a customer focus. For us, that means that it is not a long-term relationship, and it is not a profitable relationship.

So the very first step of the sales process is understanding the customer's business — their mission and their vision and what they are trying to achieve. Next, we get to the implementation phase. We do our very best to show business leaders how to create a customer-focused business. That strategy and commitment begins at the top and is communicated to the customer from the CEO level to all of the employees. Once that understanding and commitment is there, we can create a solution together with our business partners that really drives their business. It is not a one-step process. It is an ongoing process of dialog and discussion with the customer. That is what it takes to be in a really profitable customer relationship. Sometimes it takes time. If you undertake a deployment that takes much more effort and time and dollars than you initially anticipated, that can be a money losing proposition for you in the short term. However, we always persevere through those because we have selected our customers correctly at the beginning, and that always pays off in superior alignment with the customer. Not only do we help them with understanding customer strategy, and not only do we provide them with the technology to fulfill that customer strategy, and not only do we bring them the right set of partners to deploy the whole solution, but during the actual deployment we stick with them through thick and thin and demonstrate to them that we too are a customer-centered company and a customer-focused company. That process of going through a difficult deployment is also part of aligning the goals. We become even more aware of their goals, and they become even more aware of the capabilities of our technology and, most importantly, our focus on customer success and their customer success through thick and thin.

Good Technology and Great Technology

The real difference between a good technology and a great technology is the impact that it has on your customers. Does it help to drive customer satisfaction? Does it really help to increase revenues? Successfully managing customer relationships really depends on having a customer strategy. It is surprising how few companies actually think about their overall customer strategy. They go out and make a technology decision — they say, "We need some customer relationship management software, some sales force automation software, this other piece of technology," and so on. Obviously technology is a very important part of executing on your customer strategy, but the first thing that you need to do is to really understand what the strategy is and then go deploy and implement whatever technology is appropriate. If you pick the technology first, you may wind up spending millions of dollars on front office technology and actually have decreased customer satisfaction. How did that happen? The company went out and deployed something without really trying to understand the problem that they were trying to solve. Respected market research firms like Gartner report on this very topic and we encourage business leaders to study what these experts have to say.

For contact center technology, there are a few clear differentiators that make for a stellar versus a non-stellar deployment. First, how does the technology rate in terms of integration, both with other products from the same provider and with third-party providers? No company today is a homogeneous environment. All companies have a heterogeneous set of products. We have made a conscious, customer-focused decision to tightly integrate our products with each other so that they work well together from the start so our customers can quickly begin to provide their customers with a consistent experience, no matter what channel. We also integrate with numerous third-party applications, including those of our competitors, because most contact centers are multi-vendor environments. As we talk to our customers and as they participate in a multi-vendor environment and understand how well our products work together and how well our products work with our competitors' products, as often as not over time we actually end up displacing the competitors' products — not because we don't work well with the competitor's product, but because the customer now sees tremendous value in a company that is so committed to making them successful that we have invested in competing technologies. Therefore, they choose us, and they standardize on us, because then they can dramatically lower their time to deployment, their return on invested capital, and their cost of ownership because they are getting all of their products from one vendor. They can pay a single support bill. All of their internal operations are dramatically simplified. By deliberately choosing a strategy around integration with our competitors' products, we wind up winning in the long term against those competitors.

Another important point in addition to how the technologies integrate is how open the technology is. As an example, consider self-service or IVR (interactive voice recognition) which is a very popular technology due to tremendous advances in functionality and due to the fact the ROI is easily measured — which is very important in today's environment. Traditionally this technology was proprietary and not based on open standards. Today, self-service technologies based on open standards are really the best choices for long-term investment protection and immediate ease-of-use. Businesses are recognizing that because they understand that this choice will give them the most flexibility and let them quickly and affordably adapt their application to suit their customers' needs.

A number of years ago, we realized that open standards were really the way to go, and we designed all of our products to be open and standards-based. We are fully supportive of web services and J2EE and many other open standards. This keeps the costs down for our customers and makes the administration, education, and support of the products easier, and it makes integration easier. There is a much easier migration path into the future because the customer is not stuck with proprietary legacy systems. We can't emphasize enough how important openness is in today's environment because people are looking to make the most out of their existing investments. They are really looking to evolve and to stretch out the total life of every investment that they have made.

The third and we think the most important point to highlight how these technologies can be differentiated is the choice of communication platform. Businesses need an integration platform that ties together all of their communication channels, all of their data from various sources, their work force, and their tasks. They have to do that across all communication channels, regardless of how a customer chooses to make a contact, whether it is a mobile device, a regular phone, a PDA, a website, or a PC. It doesn't matter. The customer should be recognized by the system regardless of the communication channel, and enable the company to provide the right service.

One great example of this and the flexibility that is needed in a communications platform is one of our customers, Cox Communications. Despite all of the efficiencies that we brought to their operations, customers in some peak hours had to hold for longer than Cox wanted. Clearly, they could have added headcount to their support centers to handle the load, but since the load only increased at certain times of the day and the volume was somewhat unpredictable, they would have had to hire extra people who would only be really busy for a few hours a day. Instead, developed an innovative way for them to use their existing technology from us in a new way and, with their support, we actually have created a product out of our collaborative effort with them and it is called scheduled callback.

This is how it works — when the customer calls in, they get a response along the lines of, "Currently the wait times are five minutes. Would you like us to call you back in five minutes or would you prefer a call at another time that works better for your schedule? Give us the phone number that you would like us to reach you at and indicate your preferred time for a return call." This allows the company to maintain the same level of staffing, but the staff can be used more efficiently throughout the day. Most importantly, customers are ecstatic about this feature because it gives them control and shows that Cox Communications values their time and doesn't take it for granted, even if it is just a few minutes. It has dramatically increased customer satisfaction. Cox Communications benefits because they have reduced costs in three ways: they have used their available work force more efficiently, customers are not waiting on hold and racking up toll charges, and the system can allow a representative in a local area to call the customer back and thereby save further on toll charges. By being customer focused and partnering with an expert on customer-focused solutions, Cox was able to reinforce their own mission of being recognized as the best at what they do.

Unique Strategies

At our company, we "eat our own cooking." Whenever appropriate we use our own technology to do what we do best for our own customers: increase customer satisfaction, decrease costs, increase revenue, and understand customer needs. Our customer satisfaction today is at a three-year high, and our support margins have improved significantly in that same period of time.

We have been able to do that first and foremost with the use of our own technology. That is what we do best. We aim to be our best example of the benefits that we bring to other businesses. Second, we have a process for very rapid escalation of customer issues if progress isn't being made within the time specified by the service contract. Third, we encourage our customers to interact with each other and also with us as much as possible. How do we do this and what are the results? One example is our user group program. We have user groups all over the country, so our customers can meet each other, share information, and give us feedback. We have one annual conference that we invite all customers to attend. My executive team and the supportive service personnel, account managers, other key employees, and I all attend and interact with the customers. We make it lively and entertaining, with lots of educational opportunities and case studies. Our customers just love the experience because we really gear it to their needs, and we don't make it a sales call. Most of our speakers at our users' conference are our customers. Many of them are acknowledged leaders and visionaries in their field and have a lot to share with the attendees. By popular demand, even our daily keynotes are given by customers or key partners, like Microsoft last year. Of course we have one of our own keynote speakers who talks about the industry, our solution, our vision, and the state of the company, but almost all of the other presentations are detailed case studies by customers of how they have used our technology to improve their businesses. Our attendees really value what other customers have to share because they can use it to improve their own operations. We get a side benefit of increased customer satisfaction and actual cost savings because we don't have to send a lot of employees to give a lot of speeches touting our solutions. The event also creates a friendly competitive environment among our customers — we typically have people walking away saying, "We didn't know you could use that product in that particular way," or "We see that our biggest banking competitor is doing this and this and that, and we'd better catch up and start doing the same thing, because they are going to get ahead of us."

And, we walk away having learned a lot that we can continue to share with customers and use to improve our own products and services.

Another thing that I do is call customers to check in. In my opinion, all CEOs should be doing that. The personal element is very important. Often when I call back to close the loop, I actually ask customers for individual and obviously confidential opinions, not just on whether we resolved their issues, but opinions about the personnel that were involved with servicing their particular needs at that point in time, what could we have done to make service even faster and better and so on. I get some very candid feedback, and that eventually gets fed back throughout the organization. Action and changes are made as a result.

We recently hired a new chief customer strategy officer — someone who will look across our business processes and our internal processes and makes sure that everything is in alignment and that we are a customer-focused business.

We measure customer satisfaction all the time. I think most companies do that. We set new goals for ourselves in terms of improving customer satisfaction in the context of profitability. We founded a premier customer program through which long-term customers give us very honest and very regular feedback. Those people also serve as reference accounts. Then we also invite customers, both happy and unhappy customers, to speak to our employees at our all-hands meetings. The customers tell us about their experiences with us and what went well and what was not so hot and how we can fix it. Two quarters ago, we had one customer who basically said, "You almost lost me as an account. Here's why. And here is what you did that has now made me a loyal follower for life." That was very valuable because there were people from finance, sales, support, development, and marketing, all in one room and all hearing the customer say, "Here is why I nearly walked away from you as a company — because you weren't providing this, this, and this — and here is why I am here today speaking to you about how loyal I am and how you have addressed every single one of my issues, and how you have delivered above and beyond that. Now you are anticipating my needs and not just responding to them. That is what I look for in a strategic partner: someone who anticipates where I need to go and works with me to determine how to get there, rather than just reacting to my needs of today and not really understanding where the industry will be three years in the future."

Identifying Profitable Customers

Ultimate success is dictated by being customer-focused. First and foremost is doing business with companies that are themselves profitable. That is not easy today, but we really focus on successful companies, healthy companies, and companies that have a solid and broad base of their own. We look for companies that are themselves customer-focused because we don't want to be in a situation where we are scratching a current itch and the thinking is, "We have a customer satisfaction problem this year, and my CEO told me to go do something about it. We have to go out and buy something and try to deploy it. We hope the problem goes away and that we change CEOs next year." We don't want that type of customer because if we deploy our same resources at a company that is really customer-focused, then the lifetime value of that business to our business will be much higher.

Obviously financial stability is important as well. In this day and age, we have a very strong credit-checking process that makes sure that the customer is financially healthy. Most importantly, we measure the business in terms of what products we have sold each customer and what support agreements we have in place for each customer; we may lose a bit of money up-front on a product sale and maybe give them a little bigger discount, which goes counter to the way that companies run today. We do that because we are very confident that we can prove the value of our solution very quickly and that allows us to obtain a longer-term agreement with the customer. If you look at the monetary value of a one-year versus a three-, five-, seven-, or ten-year customer agreement, there is an increase in monetary value for having longer-term agreements. More and more today we focus on structuring long-term support agreements. This is unlike most technology companies that go in and sell a product and first-year support, and then they review the support agreement and hope that the client buys more support offerings. We are looking at structuring much longer-term deals with our customers that allow us to leverage our relationship over a longer period of time.

Think about what having a five- to ten-year agreement with a customer does. First of all, your competitors aren't going to call on that customer because you have a binding agreement for a very long period of time. The customer is not going to continue paying one vendor while they buy something new from somebody else. It really enhances the competitive advantage.

More importantly, it gives you the breathing room you need to really become a strategic partner to your customer. With a longer-term agreement, you not only bond the customer more closely to you for a longer period of time, but most importantly the relationship has a greater runway on which to take off for mutual long-term benefits and it gives you the space to constantly show them the value of the relationship as you build on the company's vision for their customer strategy. Therefore, they are more naturally inclined, when a new technology decision or new deployment or business issue comes up, to turn to you as a strategic partner because they have a long-term agreement and a long-term relationship with you. So they turn to you and you in turn have to make sure that you really help them with their overall business strategy. That is key.

If we find ourselves in an unprofitable situation, we tell the customer that we need to have a conversation about their support agreement; we need to structure it so that both parties are successful. For example, we have one very large customer right now that came to us through an acquisition. They had a longer-term agreement that was very advantageous to them and very disadvantageous to us. From a profitability perspective, we knew that we were losing money on this customer. We have now gone through a contract negotiation with them in which we have basically said, "Here is how much it is costing us to support you, and here is how much you are paying us. As business people, let's agree that there is a discrepancy between those two numbers, and a fairly large one. Now let's look at how many locations we are deployed at in your enterprise. Let us look at the cost savings that our products are bringing to you and the net margin contribution that we are bringing to your business. Let's look at that number. It is a much bigger number than what you are paying us or what it is costing us to support you. Let's come up with an agreement that allows us to be profitable, that allows you to be successful, and that also allows us to have the benefit of the margin contribution that we are bringing to your business." Because we understand our customers' businesses that deeply, when we have a discussion at that level, we can typically very quickly get alignment with the customer on something that no one may like, but that all will agree is a fair and equitable distribution of a value proposition. That is something that most businesses don't do. They may just continue complaining, or they may raise prices and the customer will ask, "Why are you charging me this much more? You used to charge me X last year, and now it is 2X this year." They may have an acrimonious perspective. We have a business discussion that says, "Here is the ROI that we are bringing to your business. Let's work out a situation in which we don't have a discrepancy between that and how much it is costing us to support you."

Risk

We can define risk in a number of different ways. There is technology risk, financial risk, and market risk. In terms of market and technology risk, we tend to be on the side of taking more risk than not. A number of years ago we made the very strategic decision that we would focus exclusively on open standards. That was at a time when most of our competitors were proprietary and very focused on continuing in their proprietary mode and getting another point or two of margin out of their proprietary technologies. We stepped back and said, "Let's look at the history of computing and apply that to communications technology. In the history of computing, we have seen companies like Wang, DEC, Burrows, and Univac — companies that created great products that were proprietary products and kept going with those products probably way beyond what they should have. That is the traditional crossing the chasm and innovator's dilemma that Geoffrey Moore writes about, which asks, "When do you make the bet that you need to move along to the next technology?" There are companies such as Microsoft that have totally excelled by developing the next generation technology and then moving their own installed base before anyone else can do it.

We took a look at the dynamics of computing and the dynamics of what had made Microsoft a successful company, and looked at the communications industry, and we quickly concluded that the proprietary standards were going to go the way of the dinosaur and the way of proprietary computing standards. We essentially bet the entire company on developing a next generation software platform that runs inside open data networks on open standards and provides the switching infrastructure for voice and email and web and video inside the data network. That was probably the best bet we ever made.

If you wait until you see softness in your existing business, it is too late to make the move. You are already on a downward path that only has one exit point. We made that move much earlier, and the fact that we are profitable and have been cash flow positive for the past five or six quarters is a testimony to having made the right technology and market decision and having done that through a very tough economic environment. Most companies would have said, "Let's go back to the cash cow, and let's make sure that we ride that out." The companies that we have seen do that are now out of business because they went back. There is no going back once you have hit a technology inflection point. You can only go forward. From that perspective, we have made a number of decisions that were fairly high risk, but we feel good about having made those decisions and about where we are as a company as a result of having made those.

From a financial perspective, we are very risk averse. We have a very extensive credit-check process with our customers, particularly with our new customers. We have no hesitation about taking swift action, because in this environment there are many companies that have huge receivables and huge collection problems with their customers.

Risk is very much a two-edged sword. We take balanced risks for the company, but we do that as a process of understanding the upside of taking the decision. What is the worst possible thing that could happen? We ask what the worst possible scenario would be of pursuing a given strategy. You have a very good understanding of what the total risk is because you can assign a probability to the worst possible scenario happening, and then you can take a look at what would be the worst possible thing that could happen if you don't do it, or the best possible thing. Then you make a decision between changing course or staying on the path, and the best possible outcome or the worst possible outcome. When you do that, as often as not, the answer becomes very self-evident. Sometimes it doesn't, but it is a very rare occasion when doing nothing and doing something have equivalent outcomes. If that is the case, either you haven't looked broadly enough for an alternative, or you haven't really done your analysis correctly. In my experience, in most cases, you almost always have a clear, differentiated outcome if you really focus on it and you really evaluate the risk, not just on the upside but especially on the downside.

Advice

I heard a great piece of advice from one of our customers a month or two ago. He said, "Don't focus on customer satisfaction; focus on customer success." That was a very interesting point of view. He said, "I have a lot of vendors who call me every day. I have a lot of your competitors who call me every day. They all talk about how focused they are on customer satisfaction and how they have the best customer satisfaction record in the industry, etc. But I don't really care about that. What I care about is if you are going to make me successful and if you are going to make our company successful. If you make our project and our partnership successful, I will be a very satisfied customer. But I have to tell you that I have a number of vendors today where I would rate my customer satisfaction as high or very high; nevertheless, I am going to replace them. Although their product or project is working fine and I'm happy with the level of performance they have given me, either (a) they are not strategic to me; (b) their product is a point solution that doesn't fit in with the rest of what I have, and therefore, even though I am happy with their performance, they are actually costing me money that I don't need to be spending if I have an alternate solution that maybe does less but integrates better with my infrastructure; or (c) they don't have a vision of their future that matches with where my future is. If a company is focused on customer success, to me that means that you are looking out for what my business is going to be like two years from now, three years from now, five years from now, and how you are going to help my business be successful two, three, or five years from now. If you are focused on my satisfaction, that is a today thing. I could be very happy today, but that doesn't mean anything in terms of whether you will be my partner five years from now. That is the difference between focusing on customer success, which is a long-term goal, and customer satisfaction, which can be a very transitory goal."

That is the most important piece of advice that I would give to anyone who is looking at building a profitable customer-focused business. Focus on customer success, and the satisfaction will come after.

Golden Rules

The first key to creating successful long-term customer relationships is to understand your customer's business before you sell to them. We really have to understand what the client's overall customer strategy is, where the risks to their customer base are, and what the best possible outcome or the worst possible outcome for their current customers is depending on the business decisions and customer strategy, and the best possible outcome and worst possible outcome for new customers. Once we understand all of those existing pain points and opportunity points, then we can go back in and suggest the set of solutions and technologies and processes that we can apply to take advantage of those opportunities or fix those pain points. Sometimes, it may not be a technology at all; it may be a process issue that has to be fixed inside the company.

We don't start by trying to sell our customers a piece of technology. We have a documented process within our sales organization that says, "Let's understand all of your customer interaction points. Let's understand your processes. Let's understand your pain points. Let's understand your opportunities." Once we have understood that, we then go back in and say, "Here is how various pieces of technology can create impact." It's an ROI impact in some cases. In others, it's a business benefit impact. It's a customer satisfaction improvement impact in some cases. Or it might be any combination of those. By understanding how you interact with your customers and the various organizations and people who interact with your customers, you can see how to tie that knowledge together about how you have interacted with your customers, and how you can make that knowledge available in the right format for all the other people who have to interact with that customer. Most people don't step back and actually do that or understand that you have your collections people and salespeople calling on the same customer at the same time, and you are sending mixed messages. Most companies don't think about the fact that it isn't just the salespeople calling on a particular customer; the finance group and other parts of the business are also calling. How do we tie all of those together so it is one company and one customer rather than appearing to be multiple companies with the same customer? That is where many companies fall short. They don't understand their customer strategy before they start throwing technology at a customer problem.

The second key is to understand profitability by customer. Profitability by customer isn't just how much they have bought from you recently; it is what products did they buy, how long is your support agreement, how frequently have they interacted with you on an opportunity or a problem, and have they brought value-add to your business above and beyond? So, for example, in the case of Cox Communications, the idea for the callback product actually came from Cox Communications. That added net value to our relationship. You really have to assess the overall value of a relationship from an economic perspective as well as from a strategic perspective. In the long term there has to be economic value; otherwise, there is no strategic value. You have to be willing to walk away from a situation that looks attractive on paper but the customer isn't willing to think of it as a long-term relationship. A customer relationship doesn't mean that you compromise your own profitability to provide every single customer platinum-level care at silver-level cost. It doesn't mean that you do whatever each individual wants all the time.

Customer focus is a philosophy that drives your product development, support service operations, marketing, and corporate culture. It is not a reengineering of all your processes, and it is not an introduction of all new technology all at once. In simple terms, it is really that you are clear, fair, and easy to do business with. You set expectations clearly, and you meet them. You constantly get input, and you sort out the useful and valuable input to quickly address the processes that frustrate customers. If you are committed to being a customer-focused business, then the strategies and the business decisions for R&D, marketing, operations, sales, and so forth will align with that key objective of being a customer-focused business. As a CEO, this gives me a very easy guideline for making the big decisions and the hard decisions that only the CEO is in the position to make. Finally, keep in mind that customer-focus does not mean increasing costs. There is a great deal you can do to be customer-focused. It doesn't have to cost any more in terms of labor, processes, or technology than not being customer-focused. The key point is that in the mid- to long-term, not being customer-focused enough will cost you dearly — far more than any incremental expense. It's really about an overall attitude that drives the strategy and decisions.

Let me illustrate the point with an example. Being customer-focused helped one of our valued long-term customers reduce costs and make their customers much happier at the same time. Shop at Home is one of the top home-shopping networks in the country and one of the most customer-focused businesses you can find. Customer focus drives every decision from what products they are going to offer, to when they are going to air them, to what technology they are going to use to service their customers. For example, they conduct real-time monitoring of customer response to offerings and make immediate decisions to extend the airtime of a certain popular offering or pull it off the air faster because customers aren't responding. By focusing on and knowing their customers, they have experienced approximately 40 percent revenue growth in 5 out of the past 6 years. They accomplished that because customer-focus drives their strategy. Here's what they did:

They learned that their existing customers were somewhat frustrated about waiting even a short time for a live representative and they did not want to be treated like a new customer each time they called to place an order. They preferred an automated system that would allow them to call, enter an order and quickly get off the phone or the Internet. Our society is at the stage that when automated service is easy to-use and accessible whenever we want it, we often prefer it to live service. Customers expect 24/7 service and don't mind good fast, self-service. Shop at Home very quickly deployed Aspect's self-service technology and within a week was not only saving on toll charges and overtime staff compensation but was experiencing more satisfied customers — new customers were delighted to have virtually no hold time and existing customers were delighted to have no hold-time and 24-hour access to a self-service system if they chose it over the live service. Employees could really focus on the customers that chose live service.

Exactly how did customer focus pay off? Let's look at their results.

Increased Sales

Shop At Home recognized an immediate $30,000 increase in sales the first afternoon the Aspect system was turned on. Within 2 days, a $50,000 increase per day was recorded.

Reduced Costs

The Aspect application handles a transaction in 1.57 minutes rather than the 4.04 minutes it takes to have an agent handle a transaction. With an average transaction of $200, each additional transaction handled adds greatly to the bottom line.

Reduced Abandon Rate

By combining our solution with some other applications, Shop At Home has reduced its customer call abandonment rate down to just about 3 percent or so. That is stunning! That means that most of the callers who used to change their minds, decided to call later or for whatever reason abandoned the call, no longer did so because with the new system they got immediate, focused attention and didn't have enough reason to do so anymore. Such a low abandonment rate is a highly sought after metric. To achieve it, customer-focus has to be *the* driving force behind decisions and strategy.

Do not underestimate loyalty, and do not think that spending a fortune is what it takes to create loyal customers — just think of Shop at Home — their small investment in our technology paid for itself within a week and their customers are happier for it. In closing, let me again emphasize that customer-focus as the driving force behind your business strategy will help you win every time.

Beatriz V. Infante, chairman, president, and chief executive officer at Aspect, has more than 20 years experience in creating and growing high-technology businesses, with a track record of success at companies ranging from Oracle to HP. She is the driving force behind Aspect's vision, strategy, market direction, and commitment to service excellence. Ms. Infante leads Aspect's executive team and oversees all business operations worldwide.

Creating an Emotive Attachment

Kenneth D. Tuchman
TeleTech Holdings, Inc.
Chairman & CEO

Over the last twenty-odd years, the customer management outsourcing industry has been one of robust, double-digit growth and attractive margins. Such a market cannot help but attract competition, and throughout the 1990s many small outsourcing companies entered the industry. Outbound telemarketing was the traditional entry vehicle for these companies because of the low cost of entry, readily available sales prospects, and potential for more widespread client opportunities. Additionally, contracts were plentiful, as many companies proved willing to outsource this non-core activity. As these outsourcing firms grew, many attempted to migrate up the value stream by offering more customer care- and support-related services.

These firms continued to grow, along with a strong economy and an increased customer-centric approach on the part of potential clients. Increasing competition and the downturn of the global economy, however, took its toll on the outsourcing market, forcing longer sales cycles and compressed contract values. Companies, and many of the outsourcers who service them, have taken an increasingly tactical approach to managing customer value — and they have been doing this during a time when maintaining and growing a profitable customer base is more important than ever.

Many desperate companies tried to save themselves through cost cutting and temporarily strayed from the concept of customer centricity. Despite the backlash against customer relationship management (CRM) solutions, maintaining focus on the customer is more critical today than during any time in the past. Product and service differentiation is vanishing rapidly, and in today's environment there is a direct correlation between the attention that you pay to the customer and the retention that they grant to you.

One of the most dramatic changes over the last ten years has been the increasing rate at which we have become what I call a "portable society." In the fairly recent past, the local office supply store was the only place for local businesses to purchase their paper and pens. Now everywhere from Sam's Club to Office Max provides these bulk products, even in small towns. Only a few years ago, consumers had a single choice when selecting service providers for their telephones or televisions. The regional bank was the most trusted of institutions. These geographic monopolies could be found everywhere, limiting consumer choice and opportunity to defect.

Times have certainly changed! I can change my long distance carrier without ever speaking to a person. In fact, I can even use a different carrier each time I make a call if that is my preference. With wireless number portability, one of the last switching barriers in that industry is vanishing. In both of these cases, consumers can vote with their fingers. Consolidation in financial services means I can choose from any number of national institutions, and they will offer me the same basic services. The result is consumers switching from one free checking offer to another, or transferring balances from one low introductory credit card rate to the next. Healthcare provider networks continue to expand, meaning that a patient may find the service they need at any one of many plans. Across these industries and many, many others — for both products and services — commoditization is increasing and feature sets are indistinguishable.

As a result, customer treatment is where the battle will be fought. It only takes a few bad, or even slightly negative, experiences to cause massive customer defections: service outages, poorly handled recalls, or terrible in-store experiences. Too often these things are unavoidable in the normal course of business, but without the proper customer management strategy, things can quickly go from bad to worse. Software alone cannot solve these problems. It also takes strategy, processes, infrastructure, and *real live people* — with knowledge, empathy, and proper training — to avert a customer base disaster.

Experience a few disasters, and that coveted corporate pot of gold known as "brand equity" will never be obtained. Even stainless steel brands can quickly become tarnished in this portable society. The converse is certainly just as true. I believe that there is a real opportunity to differentiate since so many corporations have taken a tactical approach to managing their customer base. If you can ensure experiences are something that allows the customer to feel a positive emotive attachment, due to a successful or unique experience, the consumer will ultimately keep coming back, in addition to going out of his or her way to share experiences with others.

For example, for a warranty interaction with an automotive organization, the enterprise should ask whether the consumer was treated like a true customer, whether he or she was trusted on the issue, how swiftly the issues were handled, and so on, as opposed to the consumer being doubted and demoralized throughout the process. If handled properly, the consumer will take advantage of the first opportunity to establish or reaffirm an affiliation with that brand.

Of course, if this were as simple as it sounds, all companies would foster customer devotion on par with Max, my eternally loyal golden retriever. So what drives so many companies so far astray? It is an unbalancing of the most basic customer management equation. There are certain tradeoffs between customer delight and enterprise profitability that a company must make with every customer management decision.

What drives the highest levels of customer satisfaction? Calls answered on the first ring by live humans. No-questions-asked return policies. One-to-one in-store employee to customer ratios. Low prices, high quality and unconditional guarantees. PhDs ready to answer consumer questions on any topic.

Certainly, high levels of customer satisfaction can increase profitability, but, except for a few niche exceptions, most companies will quickly find a point of diminishing returns where the cost of ensuring customer delight outweighs the associated shareholder return. To be safe and avoid a gray area surrounding that point of diminishing returns, most companies swing a bit too far towards the profitability side of the equation. After all, it is much easier to measure the cost of customer care than it is to measure the (sometimes) qualitative impact of satisfying customers.

Short decision horizons driven by depressed economies only exacerbate this problem. A major challenge is to create a balance between the need for immediate cost compression and the medium- and longer-term goals of strengthening and rebuilding customer relationships. For almost all companies, there is ultimately much more to be gained from managing the customer properly than there is from simply compressing cost by moving labor offshore or by introducing a piece of technology that may assist in eking out a bit more productivity. Pushing too hard on the cost compression side can make a company end up with a negative customer satisfaction outcome.

Achieving balance requires companies to take objective, thoughtful looks at themselves, their competitive environment, and their customer base. The overall plan should benchmark the company's position in the competitive landscape, where their customers' current satisfaction and loyalty levels stand in relation to the rest of the industry, and what drivers have the greatest impact to the customer relationships in such a way as to achieve the most significant bottom-line results — typically those things that help companies acquire, grow, and retain customers.

A great solution is one that addresses the questions: Is the solution going to have an impact on the acquisition of new customers? Is it going to have an impact on wallet-share growth — the ability to expand the business you have with your customers? Is it going to address the longer-term aspects of getting customers to stay with the company for a longer period of time? Many solutions do not consider these fundamental questions, and as a result, miss the mark entirely. "Point solutions" may solve any one of these challenges, but it is critical to have a holistic vision that takes into account customer loyalty, the brand impact service, the revenue impact of satisfaction, and the profitability driven by the combination of all of the above. Great solutions that consider the entire customer lifecycle can pay for themselves very, very quickly.

The ideal solution is one that manages the entire customer lifecycle. This includes customer touch points such as: prospect targeting and education; customer acquisition; customer welcome and provisioning; service and support; customer growth and development; and, finally, retention and win back. The solution strategy must take into account the systems, processes, analytics, and infrastructure required for these lifecycle categories and the many sub-components that exist within each step. Anything less leaves a gap that will result in something less than full value being extracted from a customer base.

An often-overlooked aspect of managing the customer lifecycle is the connection between the front- and back-office. Despite what may be implied by the term back-office, these operations are a critical customer interface. How much front-office traffic do back-office issues such as billing errors or incomplete claims drive? Communication and feedback between front- and back-office operations are important to optimize back-office processes, minimize front-office customer interactions, and increase customer satisfaction. Soloed operations simple will no longer work, and many companies are learning to break down the communication barriers. What is not so obvious, however, are the potential infrastructure and operational synergies that exist between these traditionally separate functions.

Certainly many back-office functions are technology heavy or require specialized infrastructure, but many others require infrastructure and resource management capabilities almost identical to those of the front-office. Workflow, systems access, and the ability to hire, staff, and manage large numbers of human resources are often common requirements. Yet many call centers stay 100 percent utilized for 1.5 shifts and sit fallow for the remainder of the day. While most call centers require real-time management of customer interactions, many back-office jobs could be completed during the second and third shifts, dramatically increasing the utilization, and thus return on investment, of those customer management assets. Any large enterprise that does not find a way to keep the call center lights on 24x7 is missing a substantial value-creation opportunity.

While front- and back-office synchronization is an often-overlooked component of a successful customer management strategy, one area that receives too much focus is technology. As bizarre as it may seem, all too often it is the chief information officer that is given the mandate to develop the customer management strategy. This is most likely a result of that crazy period of time when so many technology products and applications were marketed — by both the developers and the consultants — as the silver bullet to end all customer management ailments.

The fact is that what really dictates solid customer management is the integration of many technologies with constantly improving processes, all tied back to a strategy that delivers results. Just good technology by itself does not, and will never, deliver a result with any form of a meaningful return on investment. Conversely, just a good strategy or process, without the supporting or enabling technology, will not yield the maximum result. Once again, successful customer management is a balancing act.

There is clearly a lot of room for technology improvement, and for the most part it is much more in the ease of implementation than in the capability of the technology. There is a lot of excellent technology that, when it is ultimately implemented, can deliver on a good part of the promise that the vendors make. The problem is that the time required to customize many of these products to do what they are advertised to do is in many cases, quite frankly, not worth it. With a high percentage of technology, the speed from idea to business case to functional specification to implementation needs to be far faster than it is today.

Even if technology alone were enough, I have yet to see what I consider a silver bullet. There is such a wide variety of technologies required, including knowledge management systems, self-service systems, and predictive modeling and churn analysis systems, that no one development shop can provide a complete solution. Many of these technologies integrated together in conjunction with the right human capital, the right processes, the right technology, and the right infrastructure, however, can yield significant result. That is one of the reasons why there has been so much growth in the customer management outsourcing industry. More and more corporations are realizing that they really do not have the scale, scope, commitment, and fortitude to invest in all these different areas; they are realizing that it's a safer bet to go with someone who eats, drinks, and sleeps the concepts of optimizing profitability and delighting customers.

Finding the right partner, however, is more complex today than ever before. The customer management outsourcing industry has continued to evolve, and several key segments of competition, each with inherent benefits and risks to potential clients, have emerged:

Aggressive Pricers

These firms have reacted to the current environment by stripping out as many cost components as possible in order to offer the lowest price and a basic, commoditized service. Obviously, the benefit is a very attractive initial base price at a time when cost savings are critical to clients. The risk, however, is that these providers are forced, generally, either to take the financial punishment associated with low or negative margin — thus sacrificing financial stability — or boost margins by identifying additional billable events after a program has launched. Some providers are even forced to cut service levels drastically after the initial program launch.

Offshore Suppliers

More and more frequently, large clients are considering moving some or all of their customer management business to offshore locations such as India or the Philippines. The resulting explosion of "pure-play" offshore service providers, and the valuation premium initially demanded by these companies, has been spectacular. By working directly with these offshore companies, many U.S. clients have benefited from an enhanced "in-country" knowledge base as well as the absence of U.S. public company overhead. The associated risks include dealing with small, foreign firms; limitations in scalability, experience, and geographic diversity; and, more recently, the financial risks brought about by the plummeting valuations of these companies. Offshore companies face the additional risk of political and economic instability in many of the countries where their resources are located. Some of the recent "offshore-backlash" is a direct result of these risks.

Consultants

As increasing numbers of IT and business consultants have gained the scrutiny of a public market listing, most have sought to diversify and strengthen their revenue streams — as well as offset downturns in project revenues — through expansion into customer management outsourcing. These firms offer the benefit of robust consulting services to accompany the outsourcing arrangements, but carry the risk that as the economy improves, they may drop customer management outsourcing projects for more lucrative business consulting engagements. Another benefit is the common practice of "beachhead" pricing for customer management outsourcing as an entry vehicle to greater IT outsourcing or business consulting engagements. While this many not benefit the client business as a whole, it can offer short-term pricing advantages to the customer management organization within the client. An offsetting risk, however, may be the short tenure and limited experience of many of these companies as large-scale customer management outsourcing operators. As experienced strategists, some firms lack the tactical day-to-day expertise to manage a successful customer management program.

Innovative Service Providers

Another group of customer management outsourcing competitors has attempted to expand into value-added offerings beyond the traditional outsourcing environment. By offering such customer-centric services as data analytics, billing, technology solutions, up-sell/cross-sell strategies, and ennanced levels of quality and customer satisfaction measurement, these firms typically prioritize business solutions above all else. The benefits of these providers are their ability to provide holistic solutions that drive two key business metrics: value (revenue enhancement, cost reduction) and customer satisfaction. The risk is in the execution. Clients should ensure the provider has the experience and track record to deliver on these promises, because the cost to the client may include a higher base price — or more results-based components — with the benefits occurring through the execution of the value-added solutions.

The current confusion in the industry has driven clients to select from all four of the categories above for many reasons. The aggressive pricers typically win when business decisions are based on price alone or when aggressive pricing selection processes, such as online auctions, are employed. Similarly, offshore suppliers do well when pricing is a primary driver coupled with a client that wants simply to "test" the offshore market with a pilot program. The consultants have won outsourcing engagements from clients who are traditionally entrenched, or when an integrated IT outsourcing/customer management solution is preferable. Finally, innovative service providers find themselves serving those clients who place quality and customer satisfaction as top priorities and who are seeking a partner that can best represent them to their customers.

Innovative service providers shoulder much of the up-front capital investment required to develop their non-traditional offerings. Nevertheless, I believe such providers represent the future of the customer management outsourcing industry. The winners in this market will develop successful partnerships with IT and business consulting firms. They will develop a broad spectrum of international and offshore capabilities to best serve the needs of an increasingly global client base. They will employ industry subject matter experts and move beyond operational services to offer increased business intelligence to their clients. They will drive revenue through high standards of quality and service and manage costs effectively to keep prices competitive. Finally, they will go to market with solutions that help their clients increase customer satisfaction and promote value throughout the client organization.

The outsourcing companies that survive and thrive in the current environment have an entirely different operational philosophy than most of the companies that have flooded into the industry over the past 15 years. The foundation of this philosophy will be world-class operations and substantial experience. Success will be determined by the quick development of immediately applicable solutions — solutions that can be deployed globally, across a shared infrastructure, that promote nimble and cost-effective operations anywhere in the world.

These operations will increase flexibility and lower costs by centralizing much of the traditional call center infrastructure. The centralization will enable many of the long-awaited customer management practices such as agents at home and true call blending to locations around the world. Offshore operations will be provided at an increasingly higher quality, but offshore location will be only one component of a geographic strategy that takes into account risk mitigation, quality, time of day, language, and customer needs. World-class operations also will look at continuous improvement as a way to both decrease costs and increase quality. By tying together quality assurance, customer satisfaction, and client satisfaction, operations will have a true 360-degree view from which improvements can be implemented.

The middle tier of this operational philosophy will be the best practices and subject matter expertise brought by the provider. These subject matter experts will be able to "talk the talk" within their industries and bring true hands-on experience to the table. Along with client representatives, they will be instrumental in global governance and account management strategies that ensure a continuing partnership between the provider and the client. Finally, the pinnacle of the operational philosophy will be industry-specific solutions designed to address business challenges.

This operational philosophy also allows outsourcing partners to align the outsourcing goals with the client goals. Win-win relationships drive providers to deliver on promises, and as remuneration for living up to those commitments, have upside that is heavily performance-based. The partnership model should be focused on a relationship that is symbiotic, balanced, and designed for both parties to be rewarded based on success. It is critical, however, to define the indicators of success up front. This requires the provider to understand the client, understand the commitments, be realistic about the ability to live up to the commitments, and make sure that they are communicating reality rather than just what the client wants to hear.

The final step is to align the goals contractually. When the basic terms and conditions of the negotiation are complete, both parties should say, "Let's define in our relationship — in our contract — what the values are going to be that we're going to be measured against. What will determine that the outcome was outstanding rather than merely satisfactory?" The answers to these questions should go well beyond traditional call center service levels; they should be a means to measure true business results and should be documented clearly in the contract. It is also important to do continuous business reviews to look back and see if, in fact, the partnership is trending and tracking to outstanding overall customer satisfaction. Another way to avoid some of the conflict inherent in traditional outsourcing is to utilize a third-party company to help measure and ensure the partnership remains on track.

Most importantly, the partnership must be able to accept and operate under a changing environment. You cannot be successful in this business if you are not focused on change. The industry and latest thinking will continue to evolve, and 18 months or two years from now there will be an even more inward focus ensuring that enterprises are doing everything possible to focus on the customer. I believe large corporations will ultimately conclude that there are a finite number of customers who are the right fit for their companies. Once they come to that conclusion and realize that their customer base is one of their most valuable assets — although it is not necessarily accounted for on their balance sheets — then the path to creating emotive loyalty among those customers will appear more clear than ever before.

Kenneth D. Tuchman is a pioneer in modern customer management practices and a leading authority on customer relationship management. In 1982, Tuchman founded TeleTech, the first firm to depart from the traditional model of the teleservices industry to focus on the more expansive concept of strategy and execution across the entire customer lifecycle.

Tuchman's customer-centric approach revolutionized the industry, and TeleTech's explosive growth helped fuel a highly anticipated initial public offering in 1996. Tuchman has served as chairman of the board of directors and chief executive officer for TeleTech since its formation. TeleTech has grown to become the world's largest global provider of customer relationship services and, under Tuchman's leadership, continues its dominance as the foremost innovator in the customer management outsourcing marketplace.

It's Time for Intelligent Selling Systems

Monte Zweben
Blue Martini Software
Founder & CEO

Customer Relationship Management (CRM) software has made a lot of promises over the past decade: improved customer loyalty, smarter salespeople, increased revenue. But the technology behind most CRM systems was never designed to achieve these goals. Traditional CRM, roughly defined as "customer tracking systems," keeps the names and addresses of a company's customers in applications that are thousands of screens over databases. While centralized customer data is a very important first-generation capability, the main use for this type of system is creating reports for sales management. Salespeople simply don't like to use these systems. More importantly, these tracking systems do not engender customer loyalty, nor do they directly help increase revenue. Top industry analysts agree that the return on investment for that first wave of automation has not really stepped up to the promises made by traditional CRM.

Four years ago, Blue Martini realized the need for technology that actually engages customers, enables marketers to establish customer dialogs, and helps salespeople to sell. Intelligent Selling Systems transform the expertise of a company's best sales and marketing people into advisory applications for customers, sales people and partners. This type of software uses unique "decide and act" capabilities to monitor key customer events and transitions, propose optimal multi-channel responses, and measure the effectiveness of each response. From the customer's perspective, these types of systems actually make it easier to buy. Basically, it's like arming a company's entire sales team with the very best sales practices and also applying those practices to customer self-service.

One example of how Intelligent Selling Systems improve sales effectiveness and customer responsiveness is Hewlett-Packard. HP has solution experts all over the world that help the company map the right solution to each customer's requirements. Prior to adopting an Intelligent Selling System, it was an incredibly painful process for the company to match thousands of potential product configurations to the specific needs of a customer. However, with an Intelligent Selling System, HP encapsulates the expertise of its best solution experts and delivers this expertise right into the hands of a salesperson. Blue Martini removed the waste from that process.

If you look at the spending on sales and marketing in a company, it is extraordinarily high as a percentage of revenue. Intelligent Selling Systems dramatically reduce costs on the sell-side. For HP, it used to take two weeks to put a proposal in the hands of a customer. Now, salespeople can accomplish that in an hour. This is a new class of applications that salespeople *want* to use rather than *have* to use.

A similar scenario occurs within retail. In most stores, there are slim odds that a knowledgeable salesperson is available for high value clients the minute they step into the store. High-end retailers are deploying Intelligent Selling Systems to solve this issue. For example, Intelligent Selling Systems automate the traditional "black book" process that top sales associates use to track information about customers and serve them more effectively. This is called Clienteling. Our system is the first solution to bring the power of a centralized marketing organization together with a direct sales force to enable optimized, coordinated marketing campaigns to clients. For example, our software automatically generates a list of follow-up activities that contain targeted offers for a specific set of customers. Follow-ups can include corporate-recommended marketing actions such as in-store event reminders and special promotion reminders.

A good solution is one that helps a company get its data in order and keep track of its business processes. It allows a company to get that control in a fixed amount of time within a fixed budget. But a *great* solution is one that creates persistent and consistent best practice across the whole company. This next generation of software extracts the knowledge of the best people in the company and puts it to work everywhere to slash the costs of doing business. At the same time, it elevates the customer's experience so they absolutely want to do business with you.

Three Scenarios

Three very real scenarios for our clients follow:

1. How do you re-secure a loyal customer that has strayed to a competitor?
2. How do you identify the next wave of profitable customers before they actually fit that profile?
3. How do you increase your sales to your most profitable existing customers?

Our solutions can help address each of these areas and more. We offer systems powered by intelligent engines that help salespeople and marketers develop insights, make decisions, and take action across a broad spectrum of sell-side processes. In doing so, the expertise of the company's best sales and marketing people forms the foundation of company-wide best practices. How does this work?

Scenario 1

Our solution for relationship marketing automatically detects when a longstanding customer stops buying, and can generate a promotion to bring that customer back into the store or to a website.

Scenario 2

Our applications automatically compile data from numerous sources to create customer profiles and can pinpoint potential high-value customers, and then generate messages and offers to recruit them. For retailers, our solutions can even generate in-store messages to help sales associates identify and provide the right interactions with high-value potential customers.

Scenario 3

Our solutions provide robust up-sells and cross-sells. For example, one major chemical manufacturer is using our solutions to cross-sell plastics products across their major corporate clients, potentially worth tens of millions of dollars of increased revenue — from the same customer base.

Our clients must create profitable customer relationships. Unprofitable customers not only cost our clients sales and marketing dollars that could be spent on profitable relationships, but they can also cost the reputations of these companies. We offer technology that helps companies instantly identify their most profitable customers and tailor messages, offers, and sales interactions that are personalized for the most profitable customers. This helps companies keep profitable customers loyal. Companies can also use our technology to provide the most appropriate level of response to the appropriate customer level.

For example, one of our clients, a multibillion-dollar distributor of oncology drugs, deployed our solutions to power their website and call center. With our technology, they could identify the "high demand, low revenue" customers and direct them to a lower-cost website for self-service, while reserving the trained sales staff at their call center to handle high-potential, high-value clients. That is an ideal scenario in which the company has lowered its sales and service costs dramatically, while actually improving customer satisfaction across all customer types.

The Customer-Centric Organization

How do customer-centric companies treat their customers? Customer-centric processes are built right into the DNA of those companies. For Blue Martini, our mission is to both empower our own clients to be customer-centric, while also enacting customer-centric practices in every area of our own business. I have presented a lot on our technology, now let me discuss our business practices. Our number one priority is to understand customer needs and be responsive to those needs at every stage. For example at the beginning of a relationship, we typically perform a value assessment. What value can we provide? Not what products can we sell, but how much money can we save for our customers? How can we improve their productivity? We go through a process of determining the value of what we can do. Then we see how we can apply technology to do that. Good business partners never try and convince you to buy something from them. Rather, they become an integral part of helping to improve your business.

Going a level deeper, we typically identify a customer's significant business challenges, such as the cost of marketing or the productivity of a sales force, and we identify cost savings and revenue enhancements that we can immediately impact. We go through a financial analysis with the customer. It's a matter of both listening and educating. We can easily show the value our technology derives. But most importantly, we show how that technology can fit with their existing processes, how they can achieve that value very quickly and we produce a roadmap showing them exactly how long the deployment will take and indicate the resources required. For us, the old days of doing an "intergalactic implementation" of "pie-in-the-sky" software products are done. Blue Martini must identify our customers' key challenges, and communicate how we will meet or exceed those challenges in a finite amount of time with a finite budget.

The ideal customer life cycle is one in which we communicate our value to the market, customers identify the value we can deliver and they contract with us to get a solution up and running in 90 days or less. Then we continue to monitor this customer's success and identify new solutions that we can bring to that customer. Because of the fast success and value we bring to the table, we spread our wings as our customers automate other processes within the company, and specifically, where Intelligent Selling Systems can help. Starting with the acquisition of a company's leads and moving on to needs analysis processes and then configure-price-quote processes all the way through to the self-service processes, we address each one of these pain points individually. At the same time, we present a comprehensive road map for our customer, enabling them to leverage that technology in other business processes. The ideal situation is one through which we continually engage in delivering value to a customer, and we prove that value quickly and effectively time and time again.

I spoke of customer-centric practices as part of a company's DNA. We have done this for Blue Martini. For example, our executive team tracks the satisfaction of every single one of our customers, not just on an annual basis but on a weekly basis. Every week our services organization puts together a dashboard of every client around the world. We code each customer status as green, yellow or red, indicating our perception of their current success. We then take the first 20 minutes of an executive staff meeting in which all the vice presidents of the company are sitting around the table, and we talk about every customer that has turned yellow or red. Mind you, in most cases, we do this review prior to the customer even knowing they are considered a yellow or red. We then immediately rally any resource that is necessary in the company to turn that customer status to green. This type of process, scrutiny and pro-active customer-centric action changes the whole culture of the company and makes everyone customer-centric, No individual and no department can run from a customer problem. It is this type of process that creates true customer responsiveness and customer centricity. Customers respond to this by working with you again and again as a trusted partner. It is a relationship-building process so that when we innovate and come out with new products, customers know that they are buying products from a partner that can help make the customer successful.

Creating Profitable Customer Relationships

To create profitable customer relationships, you have to satisfy the customer and solve the customer's problem. This precept is true for our own customers and it's true for Blue Martini. Solving the customer's problem is the most important thing in the world. Everyone within an organization must be singularly focused on deriving value for the customer. If you do that, then nine times out of ten the customer will want to do business with you and you will get more business from that customer. It is simple: Just satisfy the customer. Step up to your commitments, deliver on your commitments, and derive value.

Success is a function of first setting in place a culture of absolutely committing yourself to various metrics of success and, more importantly, measuring those metrics throughout the relationship with the customer. You must have an ongoing action plan to make sure those customers are successful. Measuring where our customers are and how happy they are, and then taking action in very short order when action needs to be taken, helps us to ensure customer satisfaction. That is on the delivery side.

One of the most important things for an ongoing profitable relationship with a customer is that you have to listen to them. We don't write a single line of software code before we validate our concepts in the market. We send product managers and engineers out to both existing and prospective customers. We sit them down and show them what our vision is of where we want to go. Most importantly, we listen to the pain points and needs of our customers. We listen to their critiques of our product plans. We tune this feedback and do this over and over again with these customers until we know that the specifications of our planned products map precisely to what the customer needs. In this environment, you cannot be a technologist in an ivory tower, thinking that you have the world's answer to everything. Before you build anything, go talk to the customer and listen to what they have to say. Don't build anything until you have talked to a representative sampling of clients. There is so much technology on the IT shelves today. It is just not used because it is not useful. You have to listen. You have to be relevant. You have to offer innovative and differentiated solutions that help your own customers achieve those same objectives.

Technologies at the Forefront of the Industry

Our clients expect us to be on the forefront of delivering Intelligent Selling Systems. Companies buy solutions from vendors like Blue Martini Software because we deliver differentiated and incredibly valuable technology that maps to their business challenges. There may be larger companies to work with, in the sense of how long they have been in business and how much money they have in the bank and how many clients they have. But Fortune 500 companies continue to choose us for one simple reason: They know that our technology will enable them to achieve business objectives that they could not achieve without us. They expect us to innovate. They expect us to deliver on that innovation. We expect our customers to be participants in that innovation process. We expect our customers to tell us what their pain points are and to critique our plan of innovation. We expect them to participate actively in the road map that we are pursuing. Of course we expect our customers to measure the value we bring and be vocal about the value we bring. We like our customers to become evangelical about their success with our Intelligent Selling Systems.

Blue Martini Software Founder and CEO Monte Zweben is best known for developing and marketing highly advanced technology, including machine learning, analytics, supply-chain planning, and configuration, to some of the most well-respected companies in the world. Early in his career, as deputy branch chief at NASA Ames Research, Zweben developed automated intelligent scheduling. He then successfully applied this technology to the commercial sector when he founded Red Pepper Software, a multi-million dollar provider of enterprise supply chain management solutions, in 1992. In 1996, Red Pepper was acquired by Peoplesoft, where Zweben acted as VP and GM of the Manufacturing Industry Unit. In 1999, Zweben founded Blue Martini Software. Today,

Zweben manages the product and marketing vision and corporate direction for Blue Martini Software. Zweben's leadership and vision led Red Herring to name the company a "Top Company in the Digital Universe" and led Computerworld to name the company "One to Watch." Zweben was also named a "Marketer of the Next Generation" by BrandWeek Magazine and is a frequent lecturer, writer and spokesperson on the topic of advanced technologies in business environments. Zweben is currently on the advisory board for the School of Computer Science at Carnegie Mellon, and is on the board of directors for Advent Software. Zweben earned a master's degree in computer science from Stanford University and bachelor's degree in computer science and industrial management from Carnegie-Mellon University.

The Service Side of CRM

Sanjay Kumar
vCustomer
Founder & CEO

Providing the Service of Customer Relationship Management

In our industry, marketing is probably the most challenging thing in the world. Many companies do not want to discuss their outsourcing situation, so they don't want the providers to be talking about how we deliver an outsourcing solution to them. Thus you really cannot market your client base in a public manner. What you can market is your size, your skill, and your growth. In principle, you can market the processes that you have internally, which can be documented through various certifications, awards, and so on. The channels of marketing are trade magazines or trade shows, rather than the mass media — trade journals being more effective.

We provide solutions for companies with customer relationship issues. There are many good solutions available. A good solution is basically one that meets expectations; as a process, it is set up to deliver essentially what has been promised. A great solution is very difficult, because it requires that you go above and beyond what the client expects of you. If the client has already given you something that you think is going to be challenging in any case, it becomes increasingly difficult to go well past that. It is also very difficult to set up processes that ensure excellence, because you really have to rethink excellence every day. What was great today is not good enough tomorrow to be great. You can't rest on the same victory for too long. That's the beauty of a great solution; it's also what makes it so hard.

In terms of our own customer acquisition, there is a very clear process in place to ensure that when we attempt to acquire a customer, we do it in a very consistent manner, and we do it in a manner that we know tends to be successful. It is not simply a matter of luck — and we don't want it to be luck, because then we have not learned much about the customer. The process of acquisition is also a process of learning, and if we apply a very structured processes toward the acquisition, then we learn throughout the entire process, and we become very good at determining early on whether we will be successful or not. To ensure that we have a high ratio of successful extended interactions it is important we back off early when we know the likelihood of success is very low.

I think the best piece of advice I've heard about this business was from the Chairman of vCustomer's board Luke Helms, who once told me that "you can never outspend your competition, but you can out think them in how you acquire customers".

The Company as Client

Our clients are typically large enterprises with a significant number of end consumers who buy the company's products or services. The main reason enterprises come to a company like ours for a solution is because we have demonstrated that we understand their end customer and that we can put quality processes in place to service that end customer. We try to demonstrate in a number of different ways that we have very solid processes, we have experience, and we have the willingness to listen, adapt, and manage our people in line with our client's expectations. The biggest selling point is that we understand the value of servicing the end customer well.

How we help our clients maintain and grow relationships with their customers depends on the policies that the clients choose to implement. There are clients that really put an enormous amount of effort into developing relationships with their own end customers. In those cases, our life becomes much simpler because we can focus primarily on implementing the existing policies. We ensure that we provide the proper training to our representatives so that they follow those set policies and practices. If a client is determined to have inconsistent or inadequate policies, we spend a great deal of effort providing feedback to our clients, explaining that what we have been asked to implement will not be in the interest of their customers. We typically provide very specific examples of the challenges that we face both in a qualitative and quantitative manner. We provide clients with statistics that help them understand the issues facing their customers, like long hold times, or high levels of abandoned calls (given the staffing levels they require from us) or that the information that we have to relate to the end customers is not sufficient. These issues can all be put in front of the client, and our goal is to try to demonstrate to the client how, in a cost-effective manner, we can adapt their existing processes to give the end customer a better experience.

For each client, the underlying process is standardized, so we can use proven processes to ensure that we provide a consistent service level to their customers. We usually customize the solution, which allows us to adapt closely to our client's processes. Every client that we have has a different set of internal processes that they are imparting to us. They have a different set of goals and requirements that they are asking us to follow.

With a new client, I think the most critical step is making sure that we understand their expectations — so that we have not sold them something that we cannot deliver. Thus we spend a great deal of time helping the client understand what we will actually deliver; when our service will be ready for delivery, and how long it will take for the service to meet our client's expectation. The service doesn't start on day one at the level that the client ultimately desires, so we want to set that expectation in terms of a timeline — we set up stages along which our service will develop and improve and will eventually meet the client's expectation levels. We also try very hard to help the client identify communication channels by which our two organizations can interact with each other effectively, including escalation points, timelines according to which communications must be driven, and how we monitor our performance and service levels.

There are some very structured methods that can be used to determine success. The most common way is through a third-party audit. Say, for example, a 100 end customers have called for service, you typically know how to reach them, because the company has a phone number or an e-mail address. So a 3rd party auditing company would call or email them with a questionnaire asking them whether the interaction was useful and successful; through a series of questions they would rate that interaction on a number of levels. At the end of the day or week or whatever the designated frequency, we would sit down and analyze every single one of those surveys to understand which interactions worked well, and which ones needed improvement. We can also determine which existing policies are working, and which policies need to be revised. Whenever a customer service representative has made a certain error in terms of how they've handled a customer, it becomes very apparent through the survey. We can use the survey to provide additional training to that agent or, as often happens, a number of agents with the same problems.

Our clients expect us to be very reliable and consistent, and they want us to treat every end customer interaction with the same amount of care and diligence as if we were calling our own customers. That is ultimately the treatment we commit to giving to our clients. When we say that we will enable them to have a solution in place that they can count on they must be able to believe we will make the required effort. We are always cognizant of the fact that the revenue of our clients comes from the customers we talk to, and if the clients don't make revenue, then we don't have clients. So these customers are the reason why we have a client.

What we expect from the client is understanding and reasonableness. We want our clients to set realistic expectations of us, and we expect them to give us as much information as possible. We cannot be successful interacting with the end customer if the information from our client is incomplete. We also expect them to give us the basic tools to make us — and them — successful.

Communication and information sharing with the client is extremely important. We have taken great pains to ensure that we as the vendor have all the tools in place to ensure these communications are successful. On our website we have a client portal, which is an area that is restricted to current clients. Each of the clients has a specific section that provides various updates on their account. They can get information about where their business is headed and where our business is headed.

We have also created a monthly newsletter that goes out to all of our clients. This is simply a set of internal company articles about events that happen in the company, in terms of people, projects, and so on, including new launches and information about new clients.

In addition, I visit every client at their business location on a quarterly basis. I fly to their sites and make sure that they know we appreciate their business. We talk about new opportunities and the growth of their existing business. If you are in the business of managing client relationships, you very quickly learn that there is nothing more important than live communication. Although we talk on the phone often enough, it's a completely different relationship if you are able to meet the person face-to-face and interact on that basis.

Customer Service Issues

The three rules I try to help people implement are: (1) be honest with your customers, (2) listen to your customers, and (3) interact with your customers in a consistent manner.

I want my clients to focus on having structured processes for how they interact with the end customer, to have clear policies that their customers can understand, and to give the feeling that they care about the customer.

When you look at a profitable customer relationship, I think what you're really talking about is the ability to have a repeat customer.

Repeat customers are profitable customers. The best way to get a repeat customer is to make them believe that you care about them. Aside from the fact that you have a good product or service, you care about this individual who is buying your product. The best way to demonstrate that is through customer relationship management. There are many ways to reach out to the end customer. You reach out through communication — through e-mail, letters, phone calls (phone calls are very intrusive, so we don't recommend that method). If you have good information about your customer, you can better direct your products and services towards that customer. You can position your products and services towards that customer's current needs, and thus will create a longer term more profitable relationship with that customer.

The customer is the biggest point of feedback. Most customers are very, very transparent. If your products are not suited to their needs or the marketplace, they will let you know. If your products no longer fit their needs, they will let you know. So it's important to hear the customer and to ensure that you understand the messages that the customer is sending to you.

Customer relationships are best managed through information. The more information you have about your customer, the better you can manage the relationship — meaning manage the expectation of the customer, manage how the information about your product and service is conveyed to the customer, as well as manage how easily and effectively you can be accessed by the customer. The underlying challenge is really to make every experience of the customer a very positive one. Even if your service or your product has a flaw, if the interaction that the customer has with the company's representative is a positive one, it goes a long way toward establishing a strong foundation for the customer relationship.

We make sure that even when customers are unreasonable or incorrect in their assumptions or their expectations we still present to them the best face that we can for our clients. This often means convincing customers that they should look at how the product or service has benefited them, and telling them that we will certainly accept the feedback regarding their suggestions or expectations that were not met. You want customers to feel good about a situation that would otherwise not have gone well especially if it can be done by simply listening to them. We also make sure that customers have a broad range of information about the company and its services. We make sure that our representatives are well prepared with information, that they are very up-to-date on the company's policies and practices, and that they are not in any way misleading the customer.

Customer loyalty has to be created. It does not exist to start with. Customers will no longer give you the benefit of the doubt once they have a poor experience with your service, product or, even worse, a relationship interaction. You have to build on their experience every time they interact with your representatives as a company. One of the best ways to create loyalty is to be consistent in your approach and to always make sure you're aligning your products and services with the customers' expectations and their current requirements; to the extent that they start to trust you as a company, you are building customer loyalty. Customers tend to be very fickle once they feel that they've been cheated, as in their expectations have not been met. You could spend a long time building so-called customer loyalty, and then one mistake that goes uncorrected could bring an end to the relationship.

To help our clients gain customer loyalty, we focus a lot on consistency of the experience. We tend to have multiple interactions with the customer, and we want to make their experience as positive the first time as it is the last time. We try to ensure that they get the same information if they call up three separate times. We try to make sure our clients update the information that customers need, or have the answers to the queries they may have, or be in tune with the expectations customers have.

Loyalty and retention go hand in hand. By building customer loyalty, you are ensuring customer retention. Customer retention is not a stand-alone concept; it is merely the end result of having built enough customer loyalty so that you know you can count on customers to come back to you when they next need your product or services.

The life cycle of a customer starts with understanding the customer's needs. Once you understand a person's need, you can position your product or service to meet that need. The next step, of course, is to ensure that the customer is aware of the product or service that you are putting on the marketplace. Once a customer has decided to acquire your product or service, the important thing is to make your customer comfortable with the risk they are taking. So you want to give the customer the option of returning the product or service, or of deciding to try it at little or no risk to them.

Once the customer has used the product or service, you want to ensure that you continue to stay in touch, so it's very important that you learn about your customers and know who they are. You have to convince customers that they should come back to you with that information. You can do it through a warranty information card, which never works. Or you can do it by giving them some incentive to get in touch with you. It may be through a rebate process. Rebates are big, because people will fill in a form to get two dollars back. Online registrations have also started to become an easy way to access the customer, especially if some incentive can be provided to fill out the online information

When customers call in with a complaint of some kind, you need to take that very seriously because at the end of the day, you are learning about the customer. You learn their name, address, telephone number — whatever information is available, you want it. And at the same time, you have an opportunity to help the customer use your product or service, and if there's some fault with your product or service, the fastest way to determine what the fault is and fix it is by hearing about it through the customer. So you do need to take customer interaction through the customer service organization very seriously. Finally, I think the ultimate goal is to get the consumer to try the product or service in the future and to become a brand ambassador. And the best way for companies to ensure that is to think of every customer interaction as the basis for the next purchase.

The Role of Technology

I think the main differentiator for our solution has become the stability and the flexibility of the product. So whether it's an e-mail-based solution, a chat-based solution, a voice-based solution, or simply a backend database, at every stage the most critical piece is the underlying stability of the technology — it has to perform as advertised, 7x24. Question one needs to ask about technology: Is it really something you can trust when you put your information on it, or when you use it to contact the client? Is it going to be reliable? Is it going to be consistent? Also, these technologies need to work with other information tools or other information access points. To the extent that the technology that you're using is flexible and adaptable, you will be that much more successful in deploying it to your customer

In the future, there will be a great deal of change as the technology becomes more and more sophisticated. For example, I see customers being able to have access to a company's policies and information in a much more easily accessible manner, so they may choose not to reach out for a live interaction but to get information in a more passive manner.

Today's technology can be improved in numerous ways. The current technology is very intrusive to the customer. The customer has to call and be on hold, and wait, and provide all kinds of information. Much of this should be simplified by now, because systems have information such as your phone number, so once your phone number is put in place, once you dial a switch, that phone number should be able to activate information about how a company wants to interact with you, so you don't have to spend too much time waiting for people or a system on the other side to react to you.

Closing

The customer is king, treat him like one and they will not feel the need to look beyond your offerings. Customer service is the glue that ties consumers and providers together. As we look into the future, the customer wants live interactions 7x24 as well as anonymous web based interactions at other times. When you look to outsource your customer interaction, look for a company that has processes, technology and can show that they understand your customer.

Sanjay Kumar is the Founder and CEO of vCustomer. He is the driving force behind vCustomer's vision and ability to deliver responsive, affordable, outsourcing solutions to world renowned companies. Having provided over a dozen years of hands-on leadership to large teams at companies like Microsoft and Teledesic Corporation, Kumar brings to bear a proven management background and broad expertise in streamlining intricate processes and implementing robust technologies.

Over the years, he has chaired a number of technical groups in the area of broadband and Internet standards at the ITU, the ATM Forum, and the Winsock Forum. From developing and implementing Broadband and Internet Telephony as well as path breaking work in the regulatory framework, he demonstrates a success based risk management approach. Kumar currently serves as director on the board of the Washington Software Alliance. He holds a Ph.D. in Computer Science from the University of Pennsylvania and a B.S. in Computer Engineering and Mathematics from Carnegie Mellon University.

You Learn Everything in the Field

Jeffrey W. Dunn
Active Decisions, Inc.
President & CEO

Achieving Profitable Customer Relationships

The best way to achieve a profitable relationship is to have a long-term relationship, because if you maintain a customer over the long haul — particularly in our business model, being a hosted service — you make much more money. Longevity is clearly an important element.

You have to deliver value to these people and keep them as happy customers — referenceable customers — every day. You also have to have a win/win situation with a customer. There are certainly companies out there that don't think enough about that. We think about it a great deal; we want to get value out of the relationship, but we are hell-bent to make sure that our customer is actually getting significant value out of it. So we focus a lot on what value we're going to deliver to them, and we specifically work with them very early in the relationship to do the homework and make sure we're in agreement as to what the expectations are. We always try to put things in writing so everyone understands the goals very clearly. Some customers aren't exactly sure what's possible, so we try to work with them to make sure that things become crisp.

Our sales team and our professional services team use a methodical, step-by-step process of literally creating spreadsheets with the customers to establish what their business goals are. I think too many companies simply approach their prospects thinking the exact same thing for every customer. This is a world where success comes only

all the things they want done. Even if the customer chooses to award us only a portion of its business — a certain aspect of a project — it will know what we do and know how we can take one project and do more with it.

Our strategy is to try to create a unique offering in the marketplace. We have achieved this through a solution set that includes the construction and updating of a database, and then accessing that data and analyzing it in order to translate it into information and then into knowledge. Of course, we then apply that knowledge by creating programs from that application and then physically executing the programs, whether it is building a Web site, or doing a mail or e-mail campaign, or making and taking telephone calls. We do the execution ourselves based on each client's needs and objectives. It is a closed-loop approach, and we do all of the pieces — whether limited or unlimited by each client.

Another strategy is the use of real-time components to monitor transactions that trigger a marketing intervention. Usually, in traditional database applications, some modeling is done and then you must decide whom you will communicate to and then you communicate. Then you must wait for a return and put it back in the database, and then you can measure how well it worked. With our untraditional database applications, it is instantaneous. Somebody behaves, and they automatically receive communication. For example: If it is a bank and a deposit is made that is five times a normal deposit and above a certain dollar amount, there will be an immediate communication from the bank to that client saying, "We'd love for you to keep the money in the bank, and this is how we propose you do that."

Obviously, that's an oversimplification, but that kind of immediate communication (think of it as next day) is very different from traditional database applications. It is based on a predefined trigger mechanism, so in this case, the predefinition might be anything more than four times a traditional deposit, and a minimum traditional deposit of $10,000 makes the trigger work. And that database application, I believe, is a significantly innovative one, which we have found our customers to be excited about and which has resulted in strong ROI for our clients.

Another extension of RM capabilities with growing appeal is the use of the Web to create "marketing portals." A marketing portal is an interactive, Web-based tool used by bank branches, auto dealers, stores, agents and field sales force, etc., to enable the ordering of direct mail program pieces, e-mail and other marketing programs and collateral from enterprise-arranged sources. The portal design and infrastructure is built to meet the needs of specific companies, in specific vertical industries, and is tailored to support lines of business, branch networks and independent agents. Users customize campaigns to their immediate needs, and still do so within the guidelines and regimen of the overall enterprise or brand. Plus, in this day of ROI, just as the branch can see the local payback, the enterprise can size up and evaluate individual participation and see where it has translated into success. This is the ultimate weapon in the strategy of thinking globally and acting locally.

We try to think creatively and give our customers more than they ask for. We strive to understand our customers' customers. We set expectations in a way that helps ensure our success. The worst thing that can happen is to do a great job, but if the expectations were even greater, in effect, there is failure.

Success is what the client says it is. But unlike with many other media, what we do in a direct marketing project is easily measured — we know the cost and the returns. Success usually means we are meeting and exceeding the acquisition goal and achieving the targeted cost per acquisition, and those newly acquired customers end up growing in value and in persistence for the client.

When you look at what dictates success from an internal perspective, for our company it has to do with profit growth, increased earnings per share for our stakeholders and employee shareholders, and creating a work environment for our people that allows them to flourish.

The Role of Technology

Our perspective is highly people-intensive: A good person working on current technology will deliver more value to a client than an average person working on the next generation of technology.

Technology counts, of course, but it doesn't put a project over the top. The person working with technology toward a specific customer solution puts it over the top. And that has to do with understanding the technology and the execution of the technology, understanding the industry that the technology is applied to, and understanding the needs of the customer. And that isn't technology.

Technology is the price of entry; it's not an option. It is the enabler, but it's not the solution. It serves the strategy, not the other way around. Technology without metrics for success is almost always a losing situation.

Technology prowess is surely required, but so is training and timing of early wins, and so are implementation and the demonstration of ROI. And at the end of the day, human capital needs to be in control. Technology is just a tool of the data and marketing professional, not the other way around.

Once someone, whether it is us or someone else, has money inventing a unique, innovative, and wonderful piece of technology, we then can focus on the people side of that, and on the market orientation side of it, and on the technology *application* side of it, and that's how we make our living.

And that is not to say that we don't develop technology, because we do. It is just that technology spans the spectrum of what we do, and there are literally hundreds of technology elements that ultimately yield applications in which we specialize.

The Human Component in the RM Process

Take data quality, for example, also known as data cleansing or data hygiene. Allow me to discuss briefly our particular offering here, the

Trillium Software System®. Trillium Software System is a software solution, and is one of a few enterprise-wide data quality solutions available in the marketplace. In short, it is technology. Through an automated process, it standardizes, enhances and links elements in a marketing organization's database, or in operational transactions for use in an enterprise data warehouse, operational data store or worldwide master file. It is unique, in that it has years of application history, and ROI demonstrations that are often tenfold with clients.

However, Trillium Software System also is based on human intelligence. Its more than 200,000 modifiable business rules understand the context of data. Included are best practices that are learned from human capital, just as there are time-tested business rules identifying and linking customers, there are specific cultural and linguistic rules that enable human-like understanding of data in application specific environments. So, yes, Trillium Software can be thought of as a solution of IT professionals, but in reality, critical business applications such as RM, e-business, and enterprise resource planning suites all benefit from high data quality. Enterprise data quality, done right, is proof positive that "technology" is an enabler for the people who will make it happen.

Related to data quality is data management. Today's smart marketers are everywhere the customer is — using the medium or media of a customer's preference to dialogue, to transact, and to deliver service. Multichannel communication now comes with the territory, demanding data accuracy and customer recognition no matter what channel the customer is happening to use a particular day. Thus, we now have to ensure we have a technology in play to validate customer files so we know that they contain accurate and up-to-date contact information.

We may need to verify and enhance physical addresses so the U.S. Postal Service will deliver. We may need to correct a faulty, outdated or incomplete address, or to verify or add a valid phone number — even if the customer mistakenly provided an error. There may need to be an e-mail address validation. All this is technology at work in a marketing data center, and it is driven in part by a timely, "we need it now" demand that originates with our clients and their customers, most of whom expect immediate, relevant communication in this interactive age with those businesses with which they choose to patronize. So, while data centers deliver this quality and speed, so do the data management account teams — again, human capital — who make sure each channel of communication is optimized and that the marketing organization has a full "360-degree" view for each of its customers.

Another example is analytics. Again, analytics is now touted in many CRM software suites by software vendors — a technology-based solution. That's all well and good, but only if the user understands the discipline, capabilities, pitfalls and reality checks of segmenting customer databases, building predictive models, evaluating those models, and interpreting the results. A common plea from our clients is, "What do the data say?" and "What is the knowledge that is hidden in our data?" Human expertise — experience as a data professional, statistician and industry expert — is vital to answer these questions. It makes productive, optimal use of such software, to help derive substantive action based on accurate data reads. In effect, the software is a tool of the data professional, and not a replacement of the data professional.

Analyzing data is a specialty. Where we engage analytics with customers, for example, we do so using program development teams who interpret data and deliver solutions that make full use of the software and technology toolbox. And these teams have rich vertical industry experience. That means these professionals are adept at recognizing and avoiding "garbage-in, garbage-out" that can fault many segmentation and model-building assignments. Even a trained eye may not spot a model's deficiency until after its first test. These teams understand most diligently the build-test-read-and-refine process. Thus, once again, the most productive analytics engagements, and the unique contributions of a professional's perspective, cannot (yet) be automated fully for any one company. Technology is the enabler, not the deliverer.

Data quality, data management and multiple channel communications are and will be critically important in the foreseeable future. Also real-time monitoring to detect behavior change and the use of predictive modeling that help identify on the fly all the people who need to be communicated with is very young in its implementation. The technology of analytics is not young, but it is not old either. The IT professionals drive things, but technology increasingly will have more normative and "productionized" capabilities over time, which will be exciting to see. The IT department's partnerships with other professionals inside an organization must be strong to capitalize on these capabilities.

Customer Acquisition

Enterprises have to focus on attracting the right customers to try a product or a service. The right customers are the ones with the highest predicted future value and with the necessary propensity to be acquired.

Loyalty is about attitudes, in which we are somewhat interested. We are more interested in loyalty *behavior*. We view loyalty as an increase in loyal behavior when the share of customer is increased. It is customers coming back to spend more *and* for more things.

Purchasing behavior defines profitable and unprofitable clients. A company knows what its clients have bought, and it knows the price point at which they bought it. So then the company must dig down below to talk about what kind of profitability the customer has to the company.

A successful business has to identify the most profitable customers, nurture them, and retain them. Those customers allow a business to find look-alikes so it can begin to look for prospects from that customer base. The less-profitable customers are identified and are graduated and retained — and that is an ideal situation. The unprofitable customers are identified and hopefully graduate to profitable status. There are also unprofitable customers that will never be profitable, and an enterprise must allow them to disappear through attrition, which is very hard to do. It is counterintuitive. No one likes to lose business, but it is an important part of this equation.

In order to help our client companies acquire customers, we have to define what specifically is a best customer look-alike. Once that is done, prospects in the marketplace are identified. In our particular company, we have a complete vision of a marketing-focused data strategy: constructing and updating a database, accessing the data, analyzing the data, applying the knowledge and executing the programs. When we share this vision of what we do — this end-to-end approach — our customers don't get stuck on one aspect of a solution. They get a chance to visualize what might happen next because very often they are being exposed to the next steps. They even may learn of needs and opportunities they otherwise did not know they had — or at least better understand where their current thinking may take them. Any enterprise should seek this same complete approach to their data — and have a customer acquisition strategy for RM.

For our own company, the proportion of high-value customers that continue to do business with us defines customer retention for ourselves. As with many organizations, retention for us has to do with order frequency over time and dollar amounts purchased. Targeting high-value customers and growing a base of long-term profitable customers is the goal, as is lowering the cost of acquisition.

Some clients want to establish a vendor relationship — in other words, "Go do this." Other clients adopt a partner relationship and will sit down with us and tell us why they are pursuing the project, allowing us to help them perhaps figure out another way of getting it done less expensively and faster. It pays to know which customers are which, and to treat each customer accordingly.

The Elements of Risk

Taking risks cannot and should not be eliminated in the world of RM. When we take risks for our customers, the fact that we test and retest and test again, almost by definition says there is risk involved, but it also makes improvements on our current state.

In marketing and RM, there is hunch work, which is the risk part. And there is science, which is the reduction-of-risk part. The hallmarks of the direct-marketing strategy are measurability and accountability.

Risk taking is part of doing business. When making decisions on hiring people, a firm hopes a certain percentage will stay. In technology, a business hopes that a high percentage of the technology is optimal. Making decisions on timing and setting expectations for clients is a gamble. One makes decisions on how much risk to take to expand a business — a long-term objective — while still satisfying the short-term objective of trying to optimize earnings per share.

With respect to relationship management, risk can be minimized or managed in part by navigating with someone who has been there before, and knows how to avoid common mistakes, and understands the importance of having defined goals, the right metrics to measure objectives and a solution that is focused. In our particuiar company, we know that not many companies can say they have three decades of experience building, installing and hosting hundreds of database implementations — and thousands of data-driven primarily marketing solutions. We believe this is more than just a value-add for our clients — it's a means for them to minimize risk in their projects and assignments.

Equally important, in the RM space, is to have internal staff and external partners who are disciplined historically in direct marketing. Direct marketing's emphasis on measurability and accountability go hand in hand with today's database and RM marketing expectations. So where a pure-play software company may appear to be a reliable, stable and attractive partner, it may not understand fully the context, customization and customer demands of a particular client, in a particular industry — and the day-to-day response-driven marketing activity that must enrich the RM solution. Is the supplier going to roll up its sleeves and make it all work?

When a company is not certain if it wishes to in-source or outsource, build versus buy, or simply gain a partner who can help make RM strategies and tactics happen, these aforementioned considerations help to manage risk accordingly.

Golden Rules for Creating Customer Relationships

A sign in my office says it all: The customer is the reason we're here. You should wake up every morning believing that golden rule.

The best advice I ever received was to always do what is best for the customer even if it means we don't maximize our returns. If the client is excited by our willingness to do what it takes to make them win, they are going to be happy long-term, too.

You have to measure customer attitudes and behavior, learn from customer surveys, and understand the value equation: *trust times benefits divided by cost.*

Some people may say it's all about cost or all about value. Cost is part of value; if you lower the cost, which is the denominator, you are increasing value. But if you increase the benefits, you also increase the value, and trust is there because it is a very important component. It doesn't have as much variability, but without the trust factor being a high index number, the value deteriorates quickly.

Doing what you say you will do is a fundamental step toward establishing trust in a relationship. It's an easy thing to talk about, but it is hard to do. Trust comes from open communication and the ability to convey bad news as well as good news. For instance, instead of declaring, "Here is the problem..." try taking a "this is what we'll do about the problem" approach.

Trust comes from delivering what the customer expects, and over time you have a chance to perform. There is an ethical piece to it and an honesty piece to it, and there's an openness piece to it. In our company, these values are part of our culture, and part of our vision.

Into the Future: Evolving Customer Relationships

John Malone, a cable industry leader, once said that in five years, 80 percent of his revenue would come from sources that he hasn't even begun to offer yet. That's a provocative point of view about the pace of change and how to stay ahead of it to continue to provide value to customers.

The equation is not quite as dramatic as that for us, although it certainly does apply; we just need to be devoted to our customers and do the right things for them. If we listen hard enough, we'll wind up creating more opportunities for them, such as developing new applications for them because we have listened. We will be able to take them to a new level, and that will fundamentally change the relationship. It will allow us to work with more senior people and in more departments of our client companies.

Growth belongs to those companies that understand how to add value, and that means transforming data into information and applying it to create customer knowledge and to deliver new value based on that. In the end it also means making it happen for your customer.

Richard Hochhauser is president and chief executive officer of Harte-Hanks, Inc. — a worldwide direct marketing and targeted media company that provides a full range of customer relationship management (CRM) solutions, related direct and interactive marketing services, and regional shopper publications. In addition to his duties as president and CEO of Harte-Hanks, Mr. Hochhauser also serves as a member of the company's Board of Directors. Mr. Hochhauser joined Harte-Hanks in an entrepreneurial capacity 27 years ago. He assumed responsibility for the direct marketing business of Harte-Hanks in 1987, was named president of the parent company in 1999, and was named president and CEO of the company in April 2002.

Mr. Hochhauser has spoken at a wide range of marketing and database conferences, lectured at Northwestern, Carnegie Mellon and Rutgers, and is on the faculty of New York University. He is past Chairman of the Board of Directors of the Direct Marketing Association, served on the Advisory Board of Texas A&M University,

Center for Retailing Studies, and is currently a member of the board of directors of Modem Media, Inc., and a board member of the Center for Direct and Interactive Marketing Board of Advisors of NYU's School of Continuing and Professional Studies. Richard Hochhauser graduated from Carnegie Mellon University and received an MBA from Columbia University.

Developing Successful Customer Relationships

Charles D. Morgan
Acxiom Corporation
Company Leader

Acxiom Corporation has dual and simultaneous roles: First, we have our own customers with whom we must maintain great relationships. But the strength of that relationship depends on being able to show our customers how to get the most out of *their own* customer relationships. I call this the "show me" relationship. For our customers to enjoy real benefit from a relationship with Acxiom, we must show them how to develop successful relationships with *their* own customers.

A quick explanation of Acxiom is in order. Most companies, from small to large, collect information (data) about their customers. We believe this customer information is potentially a company's most important asset. Used correctly, this information will tell you who your customers are, what they want, and how they want it delivered. It can tell you how to cross-sell and up-sell to them, and how to prospect for new customers based on what you know about your existing customers. As your customers grow older, as their family or economic situations evolve, this data could help you keep up with their interests and adapt your marketing strategies to those changing preferences. In essence, this information can tell you how to keep your customers happy, how to retain them and encourage them to keep buying your products or services.

The unfortunate aspect is that many companies don't know how to use their customer information. In fact, they may not know how to find it because it could be in any number of incompatible databases scattered among various company locations. On top of that, the information might contain duplications or incorrect names and addresses. It's easy to imagine how many ways you can lose your good customers because of bad data. And that's not your only revenue drain. Think of the wasted expense of direct mail sent to the wrong address time and again.

That's why we believe you must use your customer information to "recognize" each of your customers, no matter how many you may have. Not only that, you should even know who your *former* customers are, and why they are no longer your customers. Then there is a multiplicity of privacy laws concerning the use of customer data that you must follow. But how do you juggle all of those tasks? The answer is called Customer Data Integration, or CDI. It takes a special kind of technology, or groups of technologies, to perform accurate and reliable CDI, but any company that is sincere about customer relationships needs to take the right steps to get the highest and best use of its customer data through CDI. That's just a fact of life in 21st Century business development.

So that's what Acxiom does: We help *our* customers establish great relationships with *their* customers. We do that by offering our customers a suite of Customer Data Integration solutions that can be adapted for the specific needs of each company within each industry. These solutions help those companies build great customer relationships and increase bottom-line revenue through customer data expertise.

Seeing Things through the Customer's View

Now that I've explained what we do, let me tell you a little about our philosophy toward our own customers. I believe that the only way a company is going to be successful in the long term is to look at things through the view of the customer. The leadership at our company has made this an essential part of our core philosophy: We must remain focused on the customer and the value we're delivering.

In each section of our company, we have a formal definition of success, including quality and performance measurements that we review with our customers on a regular basis. We instill in all of our employees (whom we call "associates") the concept that our success is our customers' success. We only succeed when customers succeed. Any time a product or service doesn't deliver value, that product or service is in jeopardy. We have to be focused on the value that we deliver to our customers. *What's promised must be delivered.*

In general, I think there are two rule-of-thumb measurements of success in customer relationships: longevity and growth. Most of our large customers are companies with whom we have developed a relationship over a long period of time — 10 to 20 years. At the same time, we have expanded those long-term relationships, providing them with new products or services, and developing new technological solutions as their needs grew and new challenges arose.

Our primary business relationships, and our most profitable customers, are with Fortune 1000 companies — the very largest banks, insurance companies, technology providers, telecommunications and retail companies in the world. Communication is a key to success with such companies, which means we work on several levels with our customers to develop those relationships. We have executive-level communication to help us clearly understand the business goals and objectives. At the operational level, a successful relationship involves more nuts and bolts, such as meeting quality- and time-related objectives. At both levels, the customers must understand what we can do well and what we should not be expected to do. We isolate issues that need correction, then follow up to ensure that the proper corrective action is taken. Throughout our work, it's important to maintain consistent, solid relationships at both the operational and executive levels.

We have to have profitable relationships. We pay close attention to customer value, customer service, and we try to see those things from the perspective of the customer. It's not what we *think* we're delivering, but what we learn from talking to the operational employees and the executives, and what we extract from our performance measurements that tell us objectively what we're delivering.

Steps for Seeking New Customers

Most of the time, our strategies to develop new customers are based on our knowledge of the industry where the customer operates. Our first goal is to understand that industry and the companies within that industry. Our second goal is to better understand the unique needs of the particular company. Often, our strategy development is at the industry level and reflects specialized knowledge. Our associates understand our value proposition in the industry and can develop a value proposition for that company that is relevant to the entire industry. We'll build a long-term plan, which will include things such as inviting customers to our executive symposiums and bringing the company executives to our briefing centers where they can see our technology up close.

For us, selling is a long-term process. Our technology often competes against ad hoc or so-called "off the shelf" products. But the solutions and expertise we've developed over the last half-century help to differentiate us. When we're engaging new customers, we start small and make sure we perform. Our goal is to develop an initial relationship through which we can demonstrate our value. Then we prove our value proposition over a set of increasingly significant engagements. We might use our diagnostic technology to show a customer how accurate the company's data is compared to an industry standard. We might augment that with products or services that would clean and update the data. We might work with only one division in a large company, to demonstrate what can be accomplished. We then grow that small relationship to other divisions within the enterprise, all of which means we have a relatively long sales cycle.

Dealing with Economic Cycles

We are in an environment in which everyone is focused on the cost side. They're less intently focused on growing their businesses, but in containing spending and maintaining revenues. Therefore, all vendor relationships — particularly those like ours that can be complex — receive a great deal of scrutiny. The intense focus on cost reduction and cost management, along with new procurement guides, are some of the most challenging aspects of our work.

It might be a cliché, but that makes it no less true: A company that is intent on delivering value to the customer will have to spend money to make money. The kinds of technologies we build and develop are often costly, so we have the challenge of proving the return on investment beyond a shadow of a doubt. There is much less taken on faith today. You have to show the customer the value, the overall benefit and prove to them they're taking little risk in making this investment. Many companies have an aversion to risk in a down-cycle environment, which means we've had to develop clear and low-risk strategies for customers to implement new technologies. We've been much more attuned to building return-on-investment types of business cases in the last few years.

What separates good and great technology is clear: it's the result you get. I can't emphasize customer results enough. Great technology generates great results at low cost and has excellent reliability and repeatability. It's a quality measure, a value measure, that will continue to prove its worth over a long period of time. The best way to judge great technology is to see how it stands out over time and becomes recognized by the people who use it.

Most of our relationships are built on standard technology components. We take the building blocks and build customized solutions. We do sell some products in a packaged manner, but those are the smaller relationships. For virtually all of our larger relationships, we custom build solutions using these standard components.

Managing the Customer Relationship

Our client companies expect us to deliver high levels of service and expect that value to be consistent. It's great for us to define value, but the only thing that counts is what the customer deems valuable. Customers are expecting better results in all their marketing channels, including traditional direct mail, point of sale, direct marketing and e-marketing. We have an opportunity to affect those results in a positive manner. For instance, in direct marketing, our experience has proven that success comes with better data content, higher quality name-and-address data and better targeting strategies. And the ROI can be measured.

But to get that positive ROI, we expect our customers to communicate with us over a broad range of expectations. For instance, we've had customers who wanted to feed specifications, and only specifications, to us without exploring the full value of what we can offer. Simple specifications fail to get to the heart of what companies are trying to do. It's difficult to judge the desired result when all you're looking at is a set of specifications for a marketing program. As we develop relationships with customers, we want to get to a level of understanding that allows us to focus on what the company can do now, how it can improve on those processes, and what it can do in the future to preserve continuing results.

Keep the Communications Lines Open

The needs of our customers and your customers are changing, just as many companies are changing. A few years ago, our customers' needs were focused on growing revenue. Now they're focused on cost reduction and growing profits. Of course, economic cycles come and go. That's why they're called cycles. As the economy cycles, companies change their needs and their focus. At the same time, their customers are changing their needs and focus. That's why I keep emphasizing that you must maintain a continuous dialogue at the operational and executive level so you are clear about how the company is maintaining its focus on the customers. Real leaders try to stay ahead of the game, to anticipate the shifting focus of both their company and their customers. It's a continuous process, but in our experience it's the only one that consistently pays off.

Charles D. Morgan is the Company Leader of Acxiom® Corporation. Under his leadership for 30 years, Acxiom has expanded from a small data processing company into a global corporation that provides customer and information management solutions for many of largest, most respected companies in the world.

Mr. Morgan has an intense interest in technology and continues to actively participate in computer programming on various projects for the corporation. By instilling a unique business culture and a vision of success, he also is one of the few executives in the country who has seen his company named five times to the coveted list of Fortune's 100 Best Places to Work For (1998, 1999, 2001, 2002 and 2003).

In 2002, Morgan joined 13 other senior executives from leading U.S. companies to form the Mailing Industry CEO Council. A non-profit organization, the Council aims to unify the mailing industry and promote the critical role that mail plays in business and commerce. He also joined the Enterprise Software Roundtable in 2002. This roundtable is a group of approximately 30 CEO's of the largest Software companies that meet to share ideas and review industry trends. Mr. Morgan also was the 2001 chairman of the Direct Marketing Association.

Mr. Morgan is a 1966 graduate of the University of Arkansas at Fayetteville, where he earned a bachelor's degree in mechanical engineering. Prior to joining Acxiom, he worked for six years as an IBM systems engineer.

Finding the Right Fit

Jeffrey Rodek
Hyperion Solutions Corporation
Chairman & CEO

Developing a Profitable Relationship

Listening to your customer is simply the most important thing you can do to build a profitable customer relationship. The second critical thing is to understand where you can add value and just as importantly, where you cannot — you have to understand the limitations of your domain expertise.

Quick returns on investment and quick wins are needed, especially during the early stages with a new customer. That way, they're winning and your winning and you're building a rapport and building success. You also have to recognize when you can and when you cannot help. For instance, if you listen and they have a pain that they thought you could solve, but you look at it and realize that you cannot help, you have to make the hard decision, the right decision, and refer them elsewhere so that they can get a solution. It may be a loss in the short term, but it is better to win their respect and do right by the customer. If you have the opportunity to say what you *can* do, maybe they will come back to you later. The alternative is to push something that is not really a fit, which inevitably is unprofitable for you and an unhappy story for the customer. This of course is no way to build a trusting relationship. Ultimately, if you have a solution for their problem, attack it and get some quick wins. On the other hand, if you don't have a fit, you have to pass on the opportunity and recommend the best company for their needs.

For example, our company can often install a new application in two or three months start to finish. With this approach, customers will likely enjoy benefits from their investment very quickly, at a time when many companies are looking to have technology investment paybacks within a year. That's what I would describe as a quick win. The customer is seeing positive returns very quickly.

In listening to the customer, you want to make sure that their requirements are understood and that their expectations are aligned with yours. There should be no communications failures. Taking the time to listen, to build requirements, to build a plan, and work the plan usually leads to success. A second challenge that we face is making sure that the employees of our company are aligned to customer success, as well as some of the more obvious goals in the company, like revenue and profits. When I worked for Federal Express, Jim Barksdale, who you probably remember from his Netscape days, was our COO. I recall being in a meeting with managers from the pickup and delivery operations of Federal Express when Jim was asked what was most important to him: cost numbers, service, or the employees. He told them if he only wanted one of the three, anybody could do it, but because he wanted all three managed, he needed talented managers like them. At Hyperion we like to think of it as the three legs of a stool. Customer satisfaction, profits, and taking care of your people are all equally important — the stool cannot stand on two legs alone.

We take that balanced approach at Hyperion. We have customer satisfaction, profit, and employee satisfaction goals. We have been working hard at this notion, especially in the past year. I have told the story about Jim Barksdale's direction repeatedly, and we've talked about the three-legged stool with our executive committee and to the top hundred leaders in the company. It is a challenge to take this concept and turn it into something that every manager understands. It is also critical that every employee touching the customer understands this idea and a picture is worth a thousand words. So, the picture of a balanced, three-legged stool helps employees keep that in mind in the heat of battle.

Communicating the company's values starts with a culture that is straightforward and honest. Help where you can help; do not help where you don't have domain expertise. You also have to be very clear in your business promise and your mission. We have worked hard, especially over the past six or seven months now, in putting together a very clear vision statement and a mission statement, on articulating our values, and defining a customer promise that can be shared with every employee in our company. Letting our customers know that we promise to deliver world-class enterprise software is imperative.

It's also important to continue to evangelize those values. I talk about our mission and our company's brand promise at every opportunity with employees. You have to evangelize inside and outside of the company all of the time and then back it up. We also talk about why it is important to raise the bar on yourself faster and higher than either the competition or your customers will. For example, think about the high jump or pole vault, two Olympic events that end in a failure. The winner keeps jumping until he or she knocks the bar down. So the winner continues to raise the bar on him or herself, higher and higher and higher. It's up to them to raise it another notch, to try again. In business, if we do a good job of listening to our customers and raising the bar on ourselves, to exceed customer expectations, we will be more successful than if we allow the customers or our competitors to raise the bar.

Hyperion and the Profitable Customer Relationship

It's important to have a clear mission, a clear promise about what your company is all about. You want to have an expectation match. Our customers are increasingly understanding that we are a Business Performance Management software company, and so when they come to us, they are looking for solutions that help them turn strategies into plans, help to monitor execution, and get insight into how they can improve both their financial and operational performance. They want help automating management processes such as analysis, planning, reporting, setting goals, modeling and monitoring results. That's what they expect from Business Performance Management. Just as importantly, you need to make it clear what not to come to us for — we are not in the business of high volume transaction processing. Other software companies do that.

Customers want to use products that work and that are from companies that stand behind them. They want to work with a company that's going to be around a long time. Therefore, they often check out your balance sheet to look at how you are spending your money, to make sure that you are reinvesting in product development. They look at your people, your products and your brand to see if there's a match. They look at all of those things to try and determine who they want to have as a strategic partner. Then they want to talk to other customers; they want references. That is the whole package of what they look for in a software company.

We firmly believe in the adage that you can't manage what you can't measure. So we survey our customers about all aspects of doing business with Hyperion. And to ensure alignment, we make sure rewards match performance vs. goals. For example, customer satisfaction is a key factor in the Hyperion bonus program. If we achieve our customer satisfaction goals, we can add bonus money to the pool. If we don't achieve our goals, we take money away. Everybody is affected and because of the way bonuses work — bonuses generally impact managers more than line employees because a higher percentage of their target compensation is bonus — it impacts our senior management even more than it impacts the front lines. You have to put your money where your mouth is. In aligning the goals, you have to measure them as the customers want them to be measured and you have to impact the reward system.

The keys to profitability in the enterprise software business are different than in many other businesses. You can achieve good margins if your selling cycles are effective, you're not doing a lot of customization, customers are implemented quickly and efficiently, and you're not selling buggy software that requires a lot of support and consulting services. But profitability is more than revenue minus cost

— you have to understand the total relationship with the customer. So we look at successful implementations and we measure how much free consulting we have to provide to ensure customer satisfaction. Another set of criteria involves how many commissions are being paid to complete a sale — is the selling process efficient, or are there too many people around and involved in a deal? And we also look at streamlining activities such as license extensions for additional users; we are increasingly turning to the Web to make those transactions both more cost efficient and also simpler for the customer.

Keeping a customer happy is as important as getting a new customer happy. We're doing this in part by putting a lot of energy into improving our support program; such as automating many support initiatives. For instance, we have about 300 customers using new software that with their permission, helps us determine the technical environment, operating system, and hardware they are using. So we short circuit a lot of the questions a support person would normally ask and get a head start on solving the customer's problem. This is easier for the customer and it makes it easier for us to give them an answer. We've learned that using this approach cuts down on customer irritation and helps us resolve a problem in a fraction of the time it used to. That keeps our costs down and the customers much happier.

The purpose of any business is to get and keep a customer. Customer acquisition is about bringing a customer into the fold and selling them software and services, but then also keeping them as a customer and growing with that customer. It is important to recognize that there is a relationship that must be kept with that customer long past the point of selling them software, whether that be further consulting work, more software or perhaps just establishing a great reference.

The software business provides a built-in mechanism to measure continuing satisfaction, since customers pay for ongoing maintenance support. In return, the customer receives updates of the software and gets help resolving any problems. Because of the maintenance contracts, measuring customer retention is pretty easy for a software company; you know how many bought your software and each month you can monitor how many are paying for maintenance to stay with you.

Customer loyalty is the step beyond customer satisfaction. With customer satisfaction, you have sold something to somebody and they are happy. In customer loyalty, they are not only happy, but they often make recommendations to others. It's very much like the old saw about if somebody goes to a restaurant and has a good experience, they might tell 10 people. If they go to a restaurant and have a bad experience, they might tell 110 people. So, customer loyalty goes beyond a satisfied customer toward a customer who is a champion, an advocate, a fanatic about what you're doing, and they're very likely to make unsolicited recommendations for you.

For example, I recently visited Yankee Stadium as a guest of NASDAQ. We were in their box along with quite a few other companies. Within my first five minutes in the box, several different people from different companies saw my nametag and affiliation, and told me how much they love Hyperion. Hearing "you've got great software!" made me feel good but it was also great for everybody else in the room to hear it, since there were probably some potential customers in the group. Another example is when I was in Pennsylvania recently to visit with a customer. The controller, a long time user of our software, said he would only allow Hyperion software to be replaced with another if it was pried from "his cold, dead hands." Fortunately losing the account was not at risk, but this is the kind of relationship that goes beyond satisfaction all the way to loyalty.

Approaching Risk in the Business

Risk — and managing risk — is very important in the software business. There are several things we do in approaching risk while dealing with the customer; such as the way we address quality assurance in product development. Ideally, you want to find any problems in the software while you're testing inside your shop, rather than finding the problems once the customer has installed it. Like many software companies, we restrict Alpha testing, or the very early, unfinished versions of software, to internal review. However we work with customers to test Beta versions, which are not quite ready for prime time but functional. By testing in the customer environment with customers who are willing to give feedback, we improve quality and manage some of the risk involved with introducing highly complex new products.

We also mitigate risk by using our own software — we call it drinking our own champagne. We have a much better sense of how the software works in the real world by virtue of our own experience with it.

Some of the work that we are doing to automate the interaction of customers also helps us manage risk. It's one thing to have a problem with the customer, but it is far worse if the solution to the problem doesn't work. That lesson was reinforced over and over during my career at Federal Express. We did not like being late or losing a package. But if we did, it could be far worse to mishandle the solution. The same thing applies to software companies. A customer calling with a problem is already upset. How that situation is handled is paramount — problems quickly resolved and with honest feedback and communication go a long way toward customer satisfaction and even loyalty. However, problems mismanaged or bungled can get very nasty. From a risk management standpoint, companies have to understand that they're going to have some problems. How those problems are resolved is the difference between world-class customer satisfaction and the also rans.

At Hyperion, the protocol for problem resolution comes through our support organization. Beyond normal call center activities, we work to contain and resolve a problem. But we also go back later and try to make sure that we've addressed the root cause rather than just the symptom.

A new change for us addresses the deployment environment. We have a deployment guide to help our people match our software to the environment and equipment being used at the customer site. In the past, we sometimes weren't aggressive enough in recommending a customer get more horsepower and a bigger machine if in fact the upgrades would have been helpful in supporting our software. But we know that customers would rather understand the requirements up front. And we know from experience in which environments our software performs best, so we should not be shy about communicating this information to customers up front. Logically, if the software works well in an environment, the chances are it will work well in a similar environment with a different customer. Communicating requirements early rather than waiting for problems to surface is a good path to customer satisfaction and part of a proactive approach to risk management.

Technology Now and in the Future

Great technology is scalable in two ways: one way is bigger, better, faster. Another dimension is in terms of making software that scales across a company and allows a great many people to use it and to collaborate with it. The Internet is a great enabler of scalable technology. For instance, our software enables thousands of users in a company to be collaborating and modeling as part of a dynamic planning process. It allows managers and knowledge workers across the company to interact with information. And it supports the notion that everybody is different, everybody has different performance indicators that they are working with. So processing speed and the ability to touch many users in a company and doing that in a way that provides data integrity and a single version of the truth are three important aspects of great technology.

We also think about today and tomorrow. A good solution meets a customer's requirements today. A great solution anticipates the future need. We talked earlier about listening to customers. There are three types of customers that you should listen to very closely. The first ones are those with the squeaky wheel. They have a problem right now; you need to listen to them, contain the problem, and go back and fix the root cause. The second type of customer is one that is interested in a very broad solution. For those, you want to go listen to them to see if you can solve their problem and close the sale. The third type is what I call the design type of customer. Design customers are really thinking beyond how today's features and functions will help them to do today's job. They can help build a vision of where your product should be in the future, which helps us decide what should be happening in our R&D labs and what should come out of the labs in three or five years.

The technology in our business is really at a magical moment. The Internet allows technology to be deployed much more widely and much more effectively, tailored to each user. The Web has simply transformed our business. You'll see companies using Web-based software to support thousands of people — all collaborating on planning, doing real-time reporting off of a single version of the truth for better financial integrity.

The Web has also enabled much broader usage of our software. For instance, for many years our software was chiefly used by finance organizations — the CFO and the controller were our best customers. With the newer Web-based technologies, we have implementations that can span the enterprise. Touching a quarter to a half of all the knowledge workers in a company with our products is a realistic goal.

Technology is a key differentiator too. We're always working for bigger, better, faster, and easier enhancements. And while there is great progress, there is also room for improvement in that area of technology. We are setting new benchmarks every year. We're improving the response times for calculating large amounts of data. And we continually advance ease of use, making the software easier to use for more people. There is no end in sight and that's just on the software side — there are huge advancements on the hardware side of it as well.

It is also important to match the technology with the needs of the customer, with what you do vs. what they need. We offer a suite of products that work together from planning to reporting to goal setting to supporting and monitoring all of these processes that we talk about, but offer customers the option of "starting anywhere." Meaning a customer doesn't have to buy the entire suite to see some immediate benefit. And this comes back to listening to your customers, having a good open dialog with them. We talk about the entire management process and some of them buy solutions to address the entire cycle. Some "get" the big picture but only want to solve an immediate pain. Still others look to enter the suite at one point, to solve an immediate and pressing need, but want to work with us to develop a roadmap to get to the bigger idea. We're ok working with our customers on each of these levels, because ultimately they have to see value and reap a benefit if the relationship is going to succeed over the long haul. Too many companies sell so hard that customers end up with more than they need…which leads to unsatisfied customers. This isn't a long-term strategy but rather a recipe for a bad reputation in the industry. If customers need everything, we're more than happy to sell it and more often than not, our customers want to take it. But one success at a time is also a good selling philosophy.

Customer Relationships in a Nutshell

In a nutshell there are five really key ideas we keep foremost in mind around profitable customer relationships.

First, perception is reality. If the customer thinks there is a problem, there is a problem. Passing the buck, as in, "it's not our problem, it is their problem or another vendor's problem," is not a successful strategy. Rather, the best companies acknowledge problems and work hard to resolve them.

The second idea is based on the reality that companies are going to have problems. Nobody's perfect. Rather, what separates the great companies is how they react and respond to problems. The great companies try to get it right as fast as they can. Then they keep at it until they've determined the root cause. They don't settle for patching over the symptoms but drive to achieve customer satisfaction.

The third idea is organized around people, processes, and systems, which are absolutely integral to customer service. It's about building a culture where those are priorities. It is also about building management systems that are built around commitment and unleashing the discretionary effort of every employee in the interest of both customer satisfaction and also profits. I think that there are things that you tell people, that you try to drill into their heads, but there are also systematic changes to make in the company. It's imperative that we instill a culture of customer service, but we also need to enable people to support that ideal. All of those things have to come together and that's been a constant mantra here.

Fourthly, companies must constantly raise the bar on themselves. The great companies are ahead of customers and ahead of competitors because they never settle, they never rest. They set very high standards and increase those standards every year.

And lastly, you can't manage what you can't measure. Customer satisfaction has to be more than just campaign slogans. It has to be just like profitability or employee satisfaction; you have to find a way to measure it. You have to go back and impact the reward system or it will probably just pay lip service to you. Everything else you need to know flows from these rules.

Jeff Rodek was named chairman and CEO in October 1999 to provide strategic leadership and direction and drive Hyperion's profitable growth. Prior to joining Hyperion, he served for five years as president and chief operating officer of Ingram Micro, the world's largest wholesale provider of technology solutions, products and services. In January 1998, while at Ingram Micro, Rodek joined the board of directors of Arbor Software, which merged with Hyperion in 1998.

Before joining Ingram Micro, Rodek spent 16 years at Federal Express Corp., a $20-billion global provider of transportation, freight, and e-commerce and supply-chain management services. Rodek's career began in Operations Research, continued in Financial Planning and Analysis, then Operations. His last position at FedEx was Senior Vice President.

Throughout his career as a provider and user of decision support and performance management software, Rodek gained an appreciation for the value of software in measuring performance and driving improved profitability.

How to Make Every Customer a Repeat Customer

Lloyd G. "Buzz" Waterhouse
The Reynolds & Reynolds Company
Chairman, President & CEO

Profitable Customer Relationships

The science fiction writer Arthur C. Clarke once commented: "Any sufficiently advanced technology is indistinguishable from magic." The problem, of course, is there *is* no magic. Only technology. Yet, what can be accomplished with technology is magical; it can make every customer a repeat customer and it can create profitable, sustainable customer relationships. But technology alone is not enough. Sustaining successful customer relationships requires a combination of people, process, *and* technology. And like one of Merlin's magical potions, if any one element is missing, the desired effect will be missing, too. At Reynolds and Reynolds, we have built our business on that principle; the lessons we have learned — and still are learning — can be applied to other businesses in other industries that serve other customers.

The three lessons we continue to learn are focused single-mindedly on making every customer a repeat customer for Reynolds and every customer a repeat customer for our customers. Here's how: (1) Invent the future with your customers; (2) Develop a passion for customer loyalty and move beyond customer satisfaction; and (3) Forget the technology — information is the new magic in profitable customer relationships.

The Market We Serve: Lessons for Other Companies

Reynolds and Reynolds is a billion dollar software and information services company that has served automotive retailing since 1927, when we first developed standardized accounting forms and processes for Chevrolet dealerships across the U.S. Today, the Reynolds brand accounts for the largest installed product base of software and information technology in automobile dealerships and the strongest market position in the industry. Reynolds serves more than 20,000 automotive retailers, every car company in North America, and delivers consulting to automotive retailers in 20 countries worldwide.

Reynolds' leadership is built on deep automotive industry experience, technological knowledge, and the unique ability to bring both together to change how our customers do business, creating value and competitive advantage for them in serving their customers. The value and competitive advantage that make our customers repeat customers is found in connecting, combining, and delivering information in new ways; ways that enable automotive retailers to manage their businesses more profitably and to serve consumers more consistently — whether within the four walls of the dealership or across the expanse of the World Wide Web.

In North America, automotive retailing is a $1.7 trillion market. With more than 25,000 new car franchised retailers, 55,000 used car retailers, 22,000 sport and recreational vehicle shops, and 53,000 collision repair shops, that marketplace generates 22 percent of all retail activity and pays more than 19 percent of all sales tax in the U.S. It is a market that encompasses dozens of players, dozens of mega-processes, and billions of transactions — richly complex and poorly connected.

The typical automobile dealer manages on average 2.3 different franchises and several distinct businesses under one roof: new and used vehicles, parts and service, sales and leasing, insurance and financing, rental cars, and increasingly, after market accessories, sports apparel, and upscale café's. Each area is information rich. Yet, automotive retailing, too, often is still characterized by islands of information and separate business operations within dealerships — different information systems and processes, different franchise reporting requirements, and disjointed, scattered touch points with consumers. Although Electronic Data Interchange has been around since the 1960s, less than 5 percent of the entire automotive value chain is connected. The opportunity to bridge the islands of information — to connect the dots of automotive retailing — is the opportunity to create unprecedented value for businesses and benefit for consumers.

We can serve that market as it exists today — delivering value, certainly — or we can invent the future of automotive retailing with our customers, creating extraordinary value by connecting the dots of automotive retailing. We've chosen to lead the transformation in automotive retailing and invent the future with our customers. For any business, building sustainable, profitable customer relationships — and making every customer a repeat customer — requires inventing the future.

Inventing the Future with Our Customers

Arthur Clarke is also credited with this notion: If a scientist can imagine a future technology, it will happen. What is technologically imaginable in automotive retailing, for instance, has, in fact, become technologically achievable and has, in fact, begun to resemble magic.

Automotive retailing has undergone more change in the past few years than in the previous one hundred. It began with consumers who, armed with new found knowledge about the vehicle they were seeking, turned the process of buying a car upside down. Today's automotive consumer is increasingly demanding, better informed, and two out of every three consumers starts the car buying process on the Web. In fact, the average consumer now visits more than half a dozen Web sites during the buying process, gathering information and impressions at each stop. They are truly informed consumers.

A decade ago, the process was simple. The consumer walked into a dealership, the dealership held most of the information, the consumer would be told the Manufacturer's Suggested Retail Price, and the consumer would begin negotiating down with the sales person's price. Things have changed. Today, the consumer interacts with the dealership on multiple fronts — the telephone, mail, e-mail, Web Site, kiosk, Telematics devices, and, yes, the new car showroom. The consumer has already done the homework *before* she (I say she, because almost two-thirds of all car buying decisions are made by women) interacts with the retailer. She knows the wholesale price, vehicle comparisons, option packages, safety record, and national averages for the make and model she is interested in. Now, the tables are turned. The sales person must negotiate up with the consumer, based on their frequently superior knowledge of the product, dealer invoice price, holdbacks, and loads of information recently gleaned from the previously mentioned sources. Simply speaking, it has become much more of a true retailing model, which is why we use the term automobile retailers at Reynolds & Reynolds. While the physical business is a dealership, what now happens in the business is retailing.

As we watched this market change in the last decade, we were reminded of an important lesson in customer relationships: It's not enough to understand *your* customer; what's required is an understanding of your customer's customer, the forces shaping their behavior, and the forces shaping the world in which both meet. It doesn't matter whether you are selling technology or sheet metal stamping machines. Knowing your customer is important; knowing your customers' customer is more important.

Inventing the future of automotive retailing with our customers is about transforming automotive retailing into a connected model — a seamless consumer experience — bringing together people, processes, and technology that change the business model for automotive retailers and the customer experience for consumers.

A glimpse of the future we are inventing with our customers begins with an electronic service reminder from the automotive retailer — generated automatically and sent anytime 24/7 — to a customer needing a 60,000 mile service. The consumer replies to the e-reminder one evening — at her convenience — using an online service scheduler, selecting the day and time that works best for her and selecting her preferred service technician.

The next morning, the service manager sees the electronic reply and the scheduled service appointment. With one click of the enter key, the service manager can check to verify that parts needed for the service are in inventory and available for this customer's appointment; if the parts were not available and needed to be ordered prior to the customer arriving for service, then the technology would have alerted him of that situation, too, and automatically generated an electronic order for the parts.

With another key stroke, the service manager pulls up a complete record of service and parts for the customer's vehicle and notices that the tires are reaching their maximum mileage life. He makes a note to discuss new tires with the customer when the car is dropped off for service. He even uses the technology to generate a percent off coupon tied to the specific vehicle and the recommended model of tires.

Next, the service manger checks another screen that displays the entire value history of this customer's relationship with the entire car dealership and sees that she and her family have been long-time customers. This prepares the service manager and his colleagues for the opportunity to treat one of their best customers with something a little extra — in the same way that retailers such as Ritz Carlton and Nordstrom respond to their best customers.

With only a few key strokes, the service manager has gained the knowledge and information that will make the consumer's trip to the service department go more smoothly and hassle free — and go further to meeting the consumer's total automotive needs. But the information doesn't stay in the service department.

Once the consumer has scheduled service, an e-mail alert is sent automatically to the sales manager's Personal Digital Assistant, alerting her that one of her best customers has made a service appointment. The sales manager checks the contacts between the retailer and the consumer — stored in a contact management data base. She reviews this customer's purchase history and vehicle interest, and takes the opportunity to follow-up on a previous desire expressed by the consumer to keep her eyes open for a convertible, if the model and pricing worked.

The sales manager greets the consumer on the morning of the service appointment, they discuss new vehicles, and the consumer takes advantage of viewing the entire new car inventory on the dealership's Web site that evening, constantly updated in real time. The consumer sees a model she likes and asks for a variety of options from lease to purchase. With the click of the mouse, different options are shown and tied directly to the car in which she has an interest.

The next day, the customer picks up the keys to her new convertible, retains her pervious car — with new tires — for her daughter to take to college in the fall, and purchases a "frequent user" card which encourages both of them to return for service.

In this ideal scenario, the unique — the "magical" — combination of technology, processes, and people delivers to the consumer the premium service she deserves, the kind of service and personal attention that can help make her a repeat customer for life. At the same time, the automotive retailer has strengthened its relationship with a repeat customer, created value for the consumer and for the dealership, and all the while has brought the consumer one step closer to being a customer for life.

Far fetched? No. Ideal? Maybe. But the technology is in place to do just that and there are automotive retailers operating in just this manner.

They Have Invented the Future — We've Simply Helped Them

The market we serve today is not the market we will serve tomorrow. In fact, the product portfolio we take to the market is heavily weighted to what the market *will* be — not what it is. It's a variation on the comment attributed to hockey great Wayne Gretsky: The secret to his success on the ice is that he skated to where the puck will be — not where it is. We are skating to where the market will be. In this market, the idea of technology, processes, and people creates new ways of selling, buying, and managing a business.

Our objective in inventing the future with our customers — the automotive retailers — is to help them grow their business, capture more revenue, and sustain higher profits. We also are helping our customers create value for their customers. It's the difference between merely providing a product or service that our customers use in the course of business, and creating new tools for the customer to use in changing how they do business and how they create value. In one case, we are meeting the customer's needs today — which is a legitimate, profitable undertaking. In the other case, we are helping that customer invent the future — which creates more value for their business, for their customers, and for Reynolds.

Support a customer's needs today and the customer may be satisfied; help the customer invent the future of his business and you may gain the loyalty that sustains a profitable relationship for years.

Developing a Passion for Customer Loyalty and Moving Beyond Customer Satisfaction

Any successful business will satisfy its customers. The truly successful — the growth companies — also will gain customer loyalty. At Reynolds, we have developed a passion for customer loyalty as a critical business and performance benchmark, which moves us beyond customer satisfaction. Customer satisfaction is still necessary, it's the ante to compete and the antecedent to loyalty, but customer satisfaction alone is no longer sufficient to sustain profitable customer relationships.

Customers can be satisfied with your product and service, yet be willing to switch to another provider who offers the next product iteration, the next feature, the next price reduction. A loyal customer has made a business judgment — a value determination — and concludes: I would choose Reynolds again. That's the key for us. A loyal customer makes a *brand* decision; a satisfied customer makes a *product* decision.

Among the customer data we collect is a focus on loyalty and specific measures on a customer's willingness to recommend Reynolds to another company and the customer's intention to continue with Reynolds. We plot "willingness to recommend" and "intention to continue" data points that create a Loyalty Index. The Loyalty Index has several advantages. It is future-oriented and predictive; that is in contrast to most customer satisfaction data, which is backward-looking. "Did the product we delivered six months ago meet your needs?" "Did we respond quickly to the last service call?" Measures that look back are useful but limited. The Loyalty Index suggests what the customer will do in the future — and, therefore, can be combined with sales data around the actual net *new* business closed with the dealership in order to gauge how well our business is performing.

We map the Loyalty Index score and measure that score against our sales efforts to introduce new technology solutions to this customer. If the customer carries a high Loyalty Index score — meaning they will recommend Reynolds to another company and they intend to continue with Reynolds — then what new business have we created with that customer? We plot where the data suggests we *should* be on these measures and then plot the actual data. If there is a gap, we ask ourselves, why? Is our incentive compensation not aligned with what we are trying to accomplish in customer loyalty? Are we not identifying the customer's needs correctly and, therefore, not offering solutions that match the true needs? Ultimately, a focus on customer loyalty has caused us to examine our business and organization more critically and to change our economic model.

Our new economic formula (our Hedgehog, to borrow a phrase from Tim Collins's wonderful book *From Good to Great*) is E = A + NS. The E is the economic driver for the company. The A is application penetration, which means the number of applications used by a single customer. For example, if Reynolds offers 200 applications, how many are being used by any particular customer? If the answer is one application, then how do we get 199 more? We'll never get all 200, because some of them are simply different alternatives, but we certainly expect to see the number of applications in our most loyal customers continue to rise. The final variable is NS, which stands for New Start. How do we get new dealerships, new car companies, new heavy equipment dealers, and new sports retailers signed up as customers? This economic model forces a dual focus and balance on increasing penetration with our most loyal customers and creating new starts with new customers. And it provides the framework within which to track the data. Simple, but powerful.

In the ideal life cycle with a customer, to build loyalty we begin with a vision of the way automotive retailing can be done — the future of automobile retailing — and illustrate how our technology and software applications can move the retailer into that future. Our value propositions to these customers are precise and driven by metrics. "Our technology and software solutions will increase your customer retention, your service capture rate, downstream revenue and profit opportunity, and improve your average repair order by x percent." Those become the business metrics the customer uses to evaluate our solutions and the metrics we use to demonstrate the return on the customer's investment in Reynolds technology. And they're not hollow claims. Each metric is tracked with automated tools and reported to the individual customer and, in aggregate, to other prospects.

In this life cycle with a customer, typically we begin with a series of base applications that demonstrate Return on Investment and the impact on the customer's business. From there, we identify additional applications — additional return opportunities — and continue to move with the customer up the value chain, from automating simple operational processes, such as payroll and accounts payable, through all of the enterprise-wide processing applications and then to more sophisticated applications and services focused on customer loyalty, retention, and Customer Relationship Management.

Finally, the other change a Loyalty Index can drive in an organization is a new look at the allocation of resources. With Reynolds' economic model and loyalty metrics, we are forced to get real clear — real fast — on where to put resources to increase business penetration with a customer, to move a customer up the value chain, to gain a new customer, or to focus on customers who are wavering on using us in the future. At Reynolds, we have realigned our organization, literally, so that the full breath of resources from across the organization — technical, human, and financial — can be brought to bear on any customer at any time to support our economic formula. That means fewer silos. Fewer artificial department lines. Fewer divisions internally. And it's driven by our economic formula. One result is, today, Reynolds has built the largest customer-facing organization in our industry. It is one more investment in long-term, profitable customer relationships, built on customer loyalty.

Forget Technology — The Magic is in the Information

The technology examples I have described can produce amazing benefits for automotive retailers. But, ironically, the technology we provide might only be a third of the solution. The technology alone is not the magic — the magic comes from the information the technology delivers, the business change the technology creates, and the process reengineering and training within the business that leverages both the technology and the information.

Reynolds provides technologies and strategies that enable automotive retailers to think differently about the information in their business and to manage it differently; transforming information into knowledge and knowledge into insight about their business and their customers, the ones served today and the ones who will be served tomorrow.

Much of the magic in information is best tapped through the alchemy of CRM tools — the new frontier in thinking differently about customers and about information. These are the software and program applications that make it possible to individualize customer relationships, build customer loyalty, and make every customer a repeat customer — one customer at a time. CRM is about information that moves a business closer to individual customers and closer to understanding their individual needs and interests. It's also about tailoring a response, a product, a service. When CRM is done well, it's the difference between simply gathering customer data and actually applying knowledge about the customer in order to change the customer's experience, making it more positive, more personal, more specific to the brand and the retailer. The idea behind Customer Relationship Management is the newest trend based on the oldest concept: know your customers and know your market. Information technology helps automotive retailers apply a bedrock concept of business to business in the 21st Century.

The art of customer relationship management was, actually, first perfected half a century ago by the neighborhood merchant. Then, CRM was face-to-face with each customer, supplemented by dozens of interactions during the week — at school, in the neighborhoods, during worship — and every conversation provided input for the merchant so that the next time an individual was in the store, all of the dimensions of the relationship would come to bear. To do today what the merchant did 50 years ago requires enormously powerful technology and business processes to match. That's what Reynolds delivers to our customers — the technologies that enable customers to tap the information that already is part of their business but that is seldom captured, integrated, synthesized or used to grow the business. With CRM tools, we show them how the magic lies in the information.

And it works. Independent research concludes that automotive retailers implementing CRM in a comprehensive manner can gain double-digit percentage increases in revenue, productivity, and customer satisfaction.

Our customers in automotive retailing — much like customers in countless other industries — are asking how best to reach consumers. With CRM, automotive retailers gain the knowledge and the ability to reach out to individual consumers in unique, personalized ways, to meet their individual needs — whether the first visit to the dealership's Web site or an electronic service reminder after 60,000 miles. The point of CRM is to make the experience for the customer more personal, more positive, and a more specific reflection of the car brand or the dealership brand.

One of the better examples of CRM is automotive telematics, the wireless technology that allows real-time communications and location information between an automobile and an information system. Telematics technologies are capable of collecting and delivering real-time automotive diagnostic and location data across a wireless network that can change the way consumers think about how their car is serviced, maintained, and protected in case of an emergency or theft. It also can change the way automotive retailers think about serving consumers, because it provides a new business model — and new technology — to use in building customer loyalty and in making every customer a repeat customer.

One such telematics technology is provided by Networkcar, which is a Reynolds and Reynolds company. Through Networkcar's small, wireless device that plugs into the standard On Board Diagnostics II port, vehicle performance data and location information are collected continuously, communicated over a wireless network to an information system, and then delivered to the car owner over the Internet on a personalized, secure Web page. The consumer's dealership service department also simultaneously receives information about the vehicle's operation and potential trouble spots.

This device can be installed by an automotive retailer or service center and will plug into 80 million vehicles already on the road and virtually every new vehicle that is manufactured. Instantly, the market for telematics and its application is expanded exponentially from the 2 million (new) vehicles sold with the service factory-installed last year. Just as instantly, there is a new business model for automobile dealerships and service centers that creates a technological link — a tether — to consumers and their cars. Finally, there is an innovation that can ease the chore of maintenance and the worry of safety for millions of vehicle owners. This is technology indistinguishable from magic.

- For consumers there are no added behaviors required: no phone calls, no activation devices, nothing more than driving the way we've always driven.
- Second, the diagnostics can deliver an early warning of mechanical failure: oil pressure that is falling or a water pump that is operating at only 50 percent capacity. The notification and data are available instantly over the Web. With cell phones now offering web access, real-time information in the car takes on a whole new meaning. The diagnostics can also perform valid emissions testing accepted by state agencies without the time and hassle of waiting at a testing facility.
- Third, if something does go wrong, you'll have GPS-accurate location information (even if your car is stolen) for immediate assistance, as well as engine performance data to understand what led to the failure and required repair. And, it's likely you'll have a higher level of trust and confidence in your vehicle service department, because you will be viewing the same information about the car as the service technician.
- Finally, since the information is delivered through a secure, personal Web site, it changes how you can think about travel by car. A family member taking a long car trip? Visit your secure Web site and view a secure map of the car's progress and location. Your college-aged daughter needs service for the car while on campus? The dealer you trust at your local service department can check and verify the problem and the repair being made hundreds of miles away.

Telematics technology applied this way has the power to change how consumers view the automobile and how automobile retailers view using technology to serve customers. It is an example of a truly connected marketplace, delivered today.

The majority of consumers with a Networkcar device installed in their automobile are twice as likely to return to the dealer for service as those without the device. Good for the automobile retailer, who has an opportunity to build customer loyalty and to improve service department efficiency. Good for the consumer, who receives better, more timely service, and is more informed about the service.

The New Magic of Making Every Customer a Repeat Customer

Information is the new magic, but it is impotent without the right technology. The right technology is indistinguishable from magic, but it, too, is impotent without the process changes that enable technology's power to deliver the magic. And both information and technology are impotent without the right economic and business model. Together all three can lead to sustainable, profitable customer relationships if you invent the future with your customers, if you move beyond customer satisfaction to customer loyalty, and if you recognize how technology turns information into magic.

In our business and in society, the future will see more technology; the technology will be more transparent, yet the impact will be more noticeable. Echoing Arthur Clarke, technology is important when it automates common tasks; technology's impact can be truly magical when it changes how we work and live. Because the point of technology is not to stop at technology, but to take the next step to magic and to ease the work of everyday living. After all, "any sufficiently advanced technology is indistinguishable from magic."

Lloyd G. "Buzz" Waterhouse has been CEO of The Reynolds and Reynolds Company since November 2002. He joined the company in May 1999 as president and chief operating officer and was elected Chairman in January 2002. He has been instrumental in refocusing the company as an information technology solutions company aimed at driving the transformation of automotive retailing.

Mr. Waterhouse has led an aggressive buildup of technology-based solutions to help automotive retailers and car companies drive productivity, efficiency and revenue growth. The company has developed and introduced solutions like the Reynolds Generations Series™, the company's next generation technology platform and a suite that integrates more than 200 applications and services to meet the needs of the automotive marketplace. Through a combination of acquisitions and internal development, the company has enhanced its strength and market share in emerging growth areas including telematics, Web services, e-business applications, and markets adjacent to the automotive industry including commercial, heavy truck, marine and power sport dealers.

Before joining Reynolds, Mr. Waterhouse spent 26 years at IBM Corporation. He has extensive experience in international business management, information technology, e-business and organizational change. Mr. Waterhouse was an early participant in the formation of the Internet. Prior to joining Reynolds, he was general manager of e-Business Services, one of IBM's fastest growing business units with annual revenues of over $2.7 billion. From 1996 to 1998 he was general manager of marketing and business development for IBM Global Services, the world's largest IT services company. He served as IBM's director of strategy during 1994-95, and was president of Asia Pacific Services Corporation, an IBM subsidiary headquartered in Tokyo from 1992 to 1994.

As co-chairperson of Dayton's e-Business Task Force, Mr. Waterhouse was instrumental in launching the iZone, which supports the birth and development of information technology-focused companies in the region. The iZone links volunteers from local businesses and development organizations with entrepreneurs so they can get advice about starting a business, obtaining funding, protecting intellectual property, finding a location and developing a business plan.

Mr. Waterhouse serves on the boards of Atlantic Mutual Companies, Pennsylvania State University's Smeal College, Fifth Third Bank, BusinessHere, ChoiceParts, i-Zone, the Downtown Dayton Partnership, Dayton Development Coalition, Dayton Business Committee, Dayton Regional Technology Council, Omega Community Development Corporation, and the Ohio Business Roundtable.

Building Profitable Customer Relationships for Business Success

William Van Symons
Clear Technologies, Inc.
President & COO C2CRM Division

Introducing CRM

We approach prospective clients hoping that they will be customers for life. Before we implement a CRM system, we walk through the business process with the customer to get a clear understanding of the benefits or value of the application. Information we seek includes how the customer runs their business, how the process works today, and what tools the company is using.

These early discussions come long before we ever show or talk to the customer about CRM or our products. The degree of information we are able to leverage, which is all integrated together, helps us understand what and how our CRM application can benefit the customer. For instance, whether the salespeople are receiving information from customer service, whether the customer service people are aware of key sales opportunities, and so on.

We walk through an initial discussion with customers to clearly understand their current processes, where there are bottlenecks, and what their potential issues and benefits are. Then we construct their "future" environment with C2 CRM and demonstrate these processes using a CRM based approach. We provide a consultant-type role with our customers, understanding their business needs and determining the best use of our CRM tool for their situation rather than just showing them a general demonstration of the product.

We build a demonstration that shows how their business is being run with the tools they have today, and we show them how those same processes would function, typically, with a higher degree of automation. They see, for example, that something that used to take an hour would now take five minutes and understand how that would benefit their users and themselves. With CRM, before making a call, a sales rep can see the support incidents that a customer has just registered. Now the salesperson can leverage that information and determine the early indicators of a customer's activity, health, and satisfaction. So before the customer becomes unhappy, he is able to take action and develop customer loyalty as a result of the way he serviced the customer in a more professional, more real-time manner.

That becomes highly profitable as the customers understand, as a result of what we're doing, how they can run their business differently with this tool. The tool enables the company to differentiate itself from the competition and, more specifically, to better satisfy its customers and conceivably enjoy 100 percent retention. The company can also continue to have a strategy to develop customers once they are acquired so they become interested in buying more products.

Another reason for the walk-through is to establish that there is a clear need, identify what it is, and make sure our solution is addressing the key customer issues and requirements. Based on what the customer tells us, we can show them how much face time and how much revenue per rep the company is getting. We actually encourage the customer to put in those metrics after the fact so it can see the value of this application. The software also enables the business process changes that we implement to leverage the tools and give service to the customer in new and different ways. It is equally important to recognize when CRM cannot address the key customer concerns. If the customers have 100 percent repeat business, the customers are all loyal, they do not need any CRM application.

Our customers expect us to:

1. Know and understand their business,
2. Make a series of recommendations based on our understanding of CRM capabilities,
3. Give them value from the CRM application, and
4. Provide the benefits they expect.

Using Scorecards to Assess Success

We measure what we put in the proposals to our customers every four to six weeks early on, and then we project future results over the life of the project. We make sure the customers have implemented the process changes and that they see the results.

The second thing we do is part of our best-practice implementation. We put together a business-process scorecard and allow customers to score themselves. There is a data-driven portion to it that says things like, "I know how much additional business I am getting," and so on.

The other portion is the process change the organization implements. The customer scores itself on the adoption rate of the new processes and new applications, and we use that scorecard as an indicator of the health of the implementation of the system. The scorecard is a process scorecard, so it is not necessarily raw data. It shows what portion of the organization has implemented the processes and bought into these processes, and judges the degree of satisfaction. We use that process scorecard as an early indicator of the adoption and, therefore, the likely success that will follow in terms of improved productivity, improved loyalty, improved revenue, and the like.

Challenges, Misconceptions, and Other Delusions

Getting customers to implement the business process change is the biggest challenge, along with making them realize that it is a tool to enable change. They must also come to recognize that if they don't enable the business process change, the tool is of little or no value.

I don't think technology is the issue; I think our challenges are in getting customers to understand how to leverage technology with improved business processes and to change the way they think when talking to their customers. The customer's problem is not that they don't have enough technology; it's making effective use of the technology but also having everyone understand the importance of "the customer" to their business.

Our longest implementation takes three months and we provide customers with something that allows them to basically use it for a dollar a day per user. It strikes me that we have wonderful technology that is very affordable — customers that want to finance the software for three years and then buy it can do that. And implementing it is straightforward for most people. So technology and cost are not problems; it is making sure our customers implement the right business processes and change their corporate culture to be customer-centric.

A great deal of information exists that isn't fully utilized in an organization. People don't suffer from lack of data. The challenge is to organize it in an effective way so people can access it and use it. It's a matter of taking a vast amount of information that exists both within a company's IT infrastructure and in publicly available sources and leveraging it for competitive advantage.

The challenge is about the process, and that is why it's important for a business to carefully select both a product and a company's expertise if they are going to get the value they expect.

The biggest misconception is that people use revenue to indicate things about customer profitability or satisfaction, but revenue is really a late indicator. It is the result of a profitable relationship. We try to make certain that customers have a lot of data in their systems, which is a good indicator of health and well-being and either their current or future profitability.

For example, if a customer calls in with a complaint about a particular product that it ordered or it has experienced a lot of late shipments, that is an early indicator that the customer is likely to be less satisfied and therefore become less profitable if left unaddressed. At that point, we want them to use all aspects of the CRM application with the customer's touch points so we can take action early rather than later.

Goal Alignment

We are in the customer-relationship business, so I want our customers to be successful in their implementations. My implementation team sets a clear mission about what it wants to accomplish in phase 1, phase 2, and phase 3. Our job isn't to get *x* million dollars in revenue; our job is to make sure the tool is successful and that the business-process changes are implemented in such a way that they can leverage the product and tool.

We start out asking many, many questions about a client's business to understand the problems it is experiencing. Our initial strategy is to focus the discussion on the company's business environment and determine what impediments to growth they may have. We determine where the customer business process needs are within the organization and the importance of that requirement to the overall business. We then develop a business process solution to address those requirements. This allows us to effectively configure the technology to address versus the traditional technology first approach.

Our initial strategy is to understand the customer's business and then develop a before-and-after model to give them a picture of "tomorrow." This allows the customer to realistically project their benefits and for us to make sure we and they have a consistent set of expectations and objectives.

To align the goals, we map our plan into a mission statement and implementation, and get the customer to agree so we are both on the same page in terms of the goals of the project and what it will reflect in the customer's business environment. This allows us to begin the project with a consistent set of objectives which is essential to the projects overall success.

Unique, Innovative Strategies

We are very focused on the mid-market, so we try not to make the plans we develop too complex. We perform what I call pragmatic best practices or business-process reviews to increase the client's chances of success. These are 1-3 days sessions designed to insure everyone understands and agrees to the business processes they intend to automate. It also helps them to clearly understand what and how to gather as well as leverage customer information for a competitive advantage.

Some pitfalls we see in CRM happen because customers think the software will do everything for them, and they fail to realize that the software will do nothing for them if it is not being used correctly. To prevent this pitfall, our strategy is to clearly define the business processes needed to leverage the tool.

Another practice that works for us is to scorecard the process every couple of weeks, which involves methodology for tracking our business practices to ensure not only that the software is implemented, but that the business-process changes that we suggested up front are in place as well. If it does not have an effective business process behind it, it is worthless.

Today's CRM Technology

CRM technology ought to involve the kinds of tools and applications that adapt to the customer's business environment — tools and applications that are flexible and mobile rather than things that require the business to change. The key is to meet the customers where they are. For example, if a client is out on the road a lot, he or she may want to have disconnected as well as Web-based use. Or maybe this client wants his or her personal digital assistant to be able to interface with the entire CRM application. Some people in the organization may be using different PDA technology and some people are sitting at a regular desktop in the office. We need to give the people in the company the ability to share information in real- time.

Because we are very focused on the mid-market, there are not thousands of people behind the scenes customizing the applications, as is the case with some of the more complex tools and products. Therefore, we think it's important for the tools to be flexible as well as usable without a lot of support people behind them.

The value is in getting the application up and running once the parameters are set to run the business. Then the executives are free to manage the business rather than spend all their time managing the computing system.

Web-based technology is key right now, as it makes it possible to access information any time, anywhere, with any device. Portable devices, such as phones or PDA/phones, are in demand for keeping in touch with customers and communicating with them no matter what devices they have.

One technology not often thought of is a connection to the back office. You really don't want to have a CRM application that is not connected to your accounting application.

Another technology that is very important is workflow which automates business processes. For us it is beyond just workflow; it is the ability to automate *when* things happen. I would like to have the system work for me, not just rely on the individual integrity of people. An integrated business process automation workflow tool automatically lets people know when important things are happening in a real-time environment rather than just hoping they discover it next time they are surfing the Web.

The Benefits of CRM

We build a lot of customer satisfaction into our dealings using the early indicators. The measure is revenue, but the indicators are usually *not* revenue. By the time revenue is affected it's after the fact.

We try to integrate something for our clients — either their customer support or their service organization. There are a series of things that encourage a customer to continue to do business, and we use those events, complaints, and applications as customer satisfaction scorecards They are indicators of the health, happiness, and satisfaction of a customer that may continue to do business with our clients and therefore have the implied loyalty that accompanies customer satisfaction. People buy from people who have done well by them in the past, so we encourage our clients to use the events to ensure that their customers are delighted with their products and services.

We check for numbers of incidents, how long it takes to resolve complaints or returns, maintenance renewals, and a whole series of indicators that are part of the customer support and service organization. They are generally what we try to implement to ensure satisfaction and to provide early-indicator measurement methodologies and growth. So if our client wants to encourage its customers to continue to buy from it, it will want a certain level of customer satisfaction to be maintained.

We usually say to customers that CRM provides three important things for their business. Normally customers think sequentially:

1. acquisition,
2. development strategy (usually they don't even know what their development strategy is), and
3. retention.

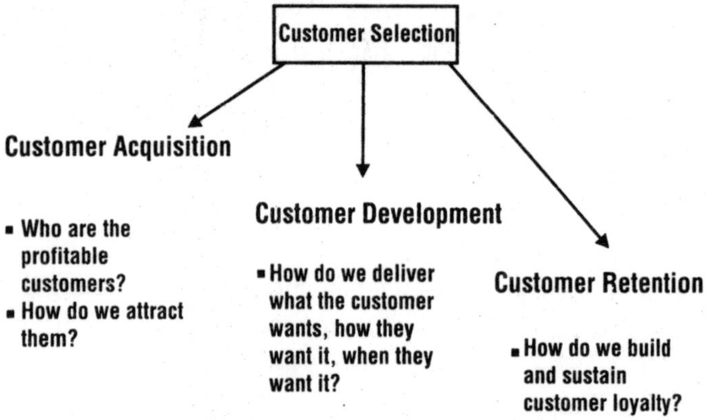

The competitive advantage will go to those businesses which manage the full life cycle relationship with their customers

We work backward for our CRM implementation. The first step in our CRM life cycle is never lose the customers we have. The second step is to ask, "What is our strategy now for developing the customers we already have?" The 80/20 rule says that 20 percent of them drive 80 percent of the revenue. We never want to lose that 20 percent. The other 80 percent fall into buckets of marginally profitable all the way to, perhaps, unprofitable. Our approach is to help our customers understand the demographics so they can leverage this customer information as a competitive differentiator. We help them develop a strategy to move customers from one profitability category to another through a series of planned actions. We help them to encourage customers in specific categories to improve their loyalty and therefore encourage more product purchasing through a series of loyalty building events. Our CRM application is then used to track these events and results so they can see the results of their activities and strategies. We use customer satisfaction as a key "early indicator" of customer loyalty and therefore buying behavior improvement. We ask our customers questions like: what kind of satisfaction, what kind of service, and what kind of products do we need to offer them as enticements in order to move them from one level of profitability to that 20 percent at the other end?

In the third stage, we compare customers to our demographics: Which customers do I want to attract? Who is in my profitable mix, and how do I find more of these for the customer acquisition phase?

We usually take customers through this process because the instant benefit in CRM is often, initially, customer retention. This provides the initial ROI that meets the customers' objective and does not require them to find new customers, just leverage the relationships they already have in a more competitive fashion.

Identifying which customers are profitable and which are unprofitable allows us to help the CRM customer focus on their high priority issues and customers first. We ask our CRM customers to review their customer turnover rate: what percentage of their customers continues to be loyal, and how many of them are lost every year? It is also critical to understand how they measure each of the items above because, in some cases, the business is using "false indicators" of loyalty. Oftentimes businesses are not leveraging all of the information within their entire business to really understand a customers' true satisfaction and loyalty — this is our goal with every CRM installation.

Often a company has only measured revenue (for satisfaction) and may have done some surveys. We integrate all of this information along with complaint, return, and customer support requests to get a "true indicator" of customer satisfaction and loyalty. We know this customer may have bought a thousand dollars worth of product from our client, but it also calls the support line a thousand times per year. We show that information graphically which allows our customers to see the revenue in relationship to cost and support.

Of course we review this with our customers and frankly most of them know the demographics in terms of certain points like "I'm looking for people between the ages of 35 and 40 who are married with two kids" — they know those kinds of demographics. What they don't know is beyond the simple revenue statement. Sometimes they haven't integrated all the other things within a business that would give those indicators — for example, they may not realize they have another set of profitable customers: the people between 20 and 25 who don't call the support center as much. They may or may not be as loyal, so we try to indicate a repeat buying pattern to show them and integrate all different aspects of the organization so our client can see not only how much revenue it is spending, but also how much time and effort it is spending in the implementation and customer support areas.

Customer Relations Advice

The best customer relations advice I ever received was to treat everybody like they are special — like they are customers for life. Every client wants to know that they are an important person to your business.

My own golden rule is to make sure I personally know my customers' business, and that I implement something for them that fundamentally changes the way they do business. It makes my CRM customers more competitive and puts them in touch with their customers.

Many businesses have what I call a field-of-dreams orientation. These businesses are actually manufacturing-oriented: They build a product and hope people will come. In the customer-centric view, we ask people what they need and want and then delight them by providing that for them. It's simple: Pay attention to the customer and build and provide a product or service that is exactly what the customer wants.

In this industrial age, we tend to be manufacturing-focused, but I try to get companies to re-architect their business to be more customer-centric. In a way, it is about managing the customer like you manage inventory. Often that requires a complete philosophical business process change along the lines of, "I am not going to build what's easy or what's next just because my engineering department wants to build it. Instead I'm going listen to the customers and let them direct me." That viewpoint is the key to growth for many clients. Some do not do that initially; they just do the retention piece where they get value. It tends to be the businesses that want to grow that adopt that philosophy.

In the future, CRM will become an integrated part of every business process. It will be inside the fabric of a business, like accounting is. Running a business in a customer-centric way will be a normal business practice. Smaller businesses may be more capable of adopting CRM because they can be more personal. It is clearly a differentiating strategy. We have found that smaller organizations can implement changes and see the benefits more quickly, and they can swiftly differentiate themselves in their markets.

Van Symons joined IBM in 1977 as a systems engineer and rose by virtue of his performance to greater and greater leadership responsibility in a series of senior marketing roles during his 25-year career with the company. In his last position, Symons directed global product line strategy for IBM's eServer. He also contributed strategic leadership to IBM's Project eLiza, a computing initiative to integrate self-managing, self-healing capabilities into the company's servers.

He received numerous awards during his tenure with IBM, including the President's Award. Clear recruited Symons in late 2002 to lead the C2 CRM team because his talent for designing software sales strategy around the needs of the customer is ideal for the mid-market, where companies demand customized solutions and a rapid return on their technology investments. Symons earned a Bachelor of Science degree in Mathematics & Computer Science from California Polytechnic State University.